SHORTCUTS TO INCREASE YOUR TYPING SPEED

SHORTCUTS TO INCREASE YOUR TYPING SPEED

Elza Dinwiddie-Boyd

A PERIGEE BOOK

To

My wonderful parents, Dave Dinwiddie, Daddy,

and Artemisa Elizabeth Baker Dinwiddie, Mother.

Perigee Books
are published by
The Putnam Publishing Group
200 Madison Avenue
New York, NY 10016

Library of Congress Cataloging-in-Publication Data

Dinwiddie-Boyd, Elza.
   Shortcuts to increase your typing speed / Elza Dinwiddie-Boyd. —
1st American ed.

       p.   cm. — (The Practical handbook series)
   ISBN 0-399-51489-9
   1. Typewriting.   I. Title.
Z49.D56   1988   88-12553 CIP
652.3'07—dc19

Book design and composition by The Sarabande Press
Printed in the United States of America
                              9   10

ACKNOWLEDGMENTS

Thank you to Adrienne Ingrum, my editor and friend, who made it possible for me to do this work; and to her capable assistant, S. Gale Dick, for his helpful cooperation.

A very special thank-you to my friend, agent, and mentor in the business, Marie D. Brown, of Marie Brown Associates, Literary Services, for her faith over the years in my ability.

This work could not have been accomplished without the loving, generous, unstinting support of my husband, Herb Boyd. Thank you, Herb, for being there for me emotionally. Thank you, Herb, for the fine editing and writing talent you lent to this project, making it what it is. Thank you for the understanding and the unfailing tenderness. I could not have done it without you!

Thank you, Edward M. Cody, master Business Education teacher, who has now joined the Superintendent's staff, Detroit Board of Education, for reading the manuscript and watching over my shoulder as the work progressed. The assistance received from my colleague and friend, Fred Hudson, of the American Business Institute, got the project off the ground. And thanks to Lisa Amoroso for her exquisite line-drawings.

A very special, loving thanks to my students at the American Business Institute and the College of New Rochelle, School of New Resources, who continually allow me to exhort them to achieve their highest potential; to Dr. Fred S. Cook, my senior advisor at Wayne State University, Detroit, who taught me how to teach typewriting; and to my dear uncle who insisted that I study business subjects.

C O N T E N T S

Introduction   11

1. The Basics   14

   Getting Started   14

   Pretest   20

   Basic Punctuation   23

   Basic Keyboard Review Practice 1   23

   Basic Keyboard Review Practice 2   26

2. Speed Development   28

   Speed Review   28

   Practice Session 1   33

   Practice Session 2   41

   Practice Session 3   47

3. Accuracy Development   55

   Accuracy Review   55

   Practice Session 1   60

   Practice Session 2   64

4. Speed With Accuracy   70

   Reaching Your Optimum Level   70

   Practice Session 1   70

   Practice Session 2   76

   Practice Session 3   82

5. Advanced Practice: *Letters and Resumes*   87

SHORTCUTS TO INCREASE YOUR TYPING SPEED

INTRODUCTION

In this, the information age, the art of keyboarding rapidly and accurately is becoming the skill which unlocks numerous doors to business, professional, and personal success. The familiar typewriter keyboard now reaches into the memory banks of computers and word processors all over the world with the simple flick of a key. Modern offices and homes increasingly rely upon the keyboard for the execution of daily routines.

There are many people who already know the standard typewriter keyboard but need to increase fingering speeds to meet the needs of America's demanding business, professional, and collegiate life. Perhaps you've just entered college and realize that you will need to produce volumes of accurate work to earn that high-honor point average needed to enter graduate school. Or, maybe you've just graduated from college and many entry-level jobs in your field require that you pass a typing-speed test. Or, perhaps to get that promotion you want so badly you will need speed and accuracy in keyboarding. It could be that you are planning to return to work after several years of parenting.

If you want to build keyboard speed quickly and accurately, if you wish to compete in an age in which the importance of computers and word processors, which use the standard typewriter keyboard, grows larger everyday, and if you have learned the standard typewriter keyboard but wish to increase your speed, whether to write a book or get a job—this book is for you.

Speed is not a by-product of any particular skill; producing work day after day does not build speed. Speed requires specific practice and techniques. This book will focus your attention on building speed at the keyboard. Following the plan of this book will allow you to develop high speeds without sacrificing accuracy.

Skill development in keyboarding is akin to skill development in any other field. Skill has to evolve and be refined. This book will teach you lesson by lesson how to type faster and gain control so that you obtain maximum speed at peak accuracy. And *Shortcuts to Increase Your Typing Speed* will show you how to refine your keyboarding speed *quickly*, in as little as 10 days.

While this book is based on the good thinking and good practice of many experts in the field today, the key to its effectiveness is you. Success is nearly always a direct result of motivation and commitment. People with moderate talent who have high levels of motivation, commitment, constructive self-criticism, and discipline can easily out perform people of extraordinary talent and low motivation. If *Shortcuts to Increase Your Typing Speed* is to help you build maximum speed and accuracy in a short period of time, you must be motivated and committed. This cannot be overstressed.

Be a self-prodder, since speed requires constant self-prodding. It also requires goal setting and disciplined accomplishment. So set goals and use proper technique and practice. Employ the basic imperatives for speed outlined here and watch your keyboarding skill develop. Concentration is fundamental to both speed and accuracy. When your mind wanders, bring it back and concentrate on the job at hand. Know

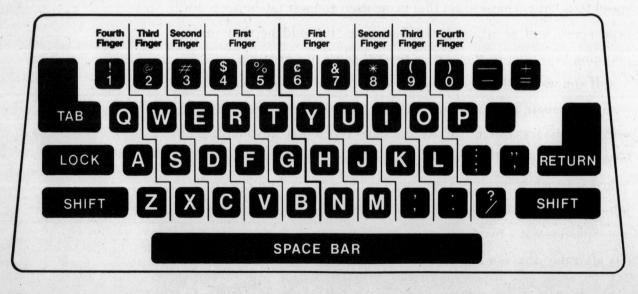

proper technique and concentrate on it until it becomes an automatic reflex.

The modern keyboard—microcomputer, word processor, electronic typewriter, or standard electric typewriter—is easier to master than the manual keyboard. The new, more flattened model provides closer key banks. There are not steps to climb as in the old manual and early electric typewriters. Numbers and symbols are more accessible and present fewer reach problems.

Throughout the work you will find helpful hints on the art of success while you increase your typing speed. Since motivation is the prime requirement, *Shortcuts to Increase Your Typing Speed* encompasses a motivational quality to assist you in right thinking as you pursue your goals.

As you work through the drills, remember: *Shortcuts to Increase Your Typing Speed* is a book on self-discipline. It invites you to indulge in the supreme rewards of self-education.

O N E

THE BASICS

GETTING STARTED

Before you go any further, it is important that you already know the basic typewriter keyboard. It doesn't matter how long ago you learned or how short your course of study, but you should be familiar with the keyboard. If after the pretest you find that you are beginning with the Basic Keyboard Review on p. 23, be aware that that section is a review of the keyboard; it is not an introduction to the keyboard! Each lesson assumes that you know the alphabet and number keyboard by memory and wish to build your speed.

First, evaluate the level of your commitment and motivation. You need to judge correctly the degree of intensity you are bringing to this project; your results will correspond directly to your commitment and motivation. You may be a long-range planner, a person who looks to the future and gets ready for it. Or, have you just learned that to get that job you want so badly you will need to pass a typing test within two weeks? The amount of practice time you allow will be determined by your time frame. Frequency and length of practice will correspond directly to your motivation. Best results are achieved by regular practice sessions—daily if possible—of at least one hour.

After you are clear about your motivation and commitment, set up a practice schedule that complements it, one you can follow consistently. If you want to make significant progress in two weeks, you need to practice at least two hours every day. In order to build your stamina, you might begin with half-hour sessions, increasing the time by 10 minutes each succeeding session until you have reached the one-hour mark. If you are aiming for two hours, when you reach the one-hour point increase the sessions by 15–20 minutes per session until you are putting in 120 minutes of practice time.

If you complete all of the drills in the lesson before the time is up, do the drills a second time, this time concentrating on those words that gave you the most trouble. Use any remaining time to return to previous sessions and practice drill lines that you have not yet mastered until you have them down pat.

Remember: Good skill building is based on good practice. Beware of practicing when you are tired. You can do more harm this way than good. Schedule your practice sessions for periods when you feel most fresh and alert. Early morning practice, following adequate rest, can come before or after a light breakfast. Whatever time of day you select to practice, remember: Bad practice harms development. Plan your practice sessions when you are well rested.

Find a quiet, well lit, permanent spot to set up your workstation. Post your practice schedule in plain view and adhere to it. You will need a timer for many of the drills in this book. You can use a typical kitchen timer, or any timer that you can set easily and that will ring loud enough to get your attention.

As you know, concentration is one key to the success of this plan. Begin your practice of concentrating by keeping to your work schedule. After a few days, review its effectiveness, making adjustments as needed. Remember: Regularity is basic to skill building.

Organization is a key component of concentration. Arrange your work area for maximum efficiency. Maintain a neat and orderly workplace, freeing your desk of clutter, of all unnecessary books and other paraphernalia. Keep all of your materials in the work area. Place your book in an upright position, tilted slightly backward for easy reading. Many office-supply stores sell gadgets for upright placement of copy to be keyboarded. Keep your timer in easy reach. If you are using a standard electric typewriter, or an electronic typewriter, place a ready supply of typing paper near the edge of the table or desk to the left of the typewriter. Practice inserting your paper quickly, with one swift motion.

The front frame of your keyboard should be even with the front edge of the desk. When you finish a session, restore your work area to its former state of orderliness.

It will pay to review the major components of your typewriter or word processor. If you are working with a typewriter, before beginning each lesson adjust your paper guide so that it lines up with zero (0) on the paper-bail scale (used to measure the number of characters per inch) or the margin scale. Grasp the left edge of your paper with your left hand and align it with the left edge of the paper guide. With a quick flick of the right platen knob (knob that moves the roller) or index key (which causes the roller to move automatically), turn the paper quickly into the machine. Straighten the paper if necessary. Practice this to achieve smooth, quick paper insertion.

If you are practicing on a word processor, electronic typewriter, or microcomputer, you will need to review the beginning instructions in your owner's manual. When keyboarding on a video display terminal (VDT) or cathrode ray tube (CRT), you may adjust the brightness and contrast. Your manual will instruct you in the use of the special code keys, including delete and tabulator keys. It will also explain document layout which includes margin setting. When you have inserted your diskette in the disk drive, follow the instructions given on the menu. Whether you are using a typewriter or computer, set your margins for a line which will allow 70 spaces per line for the drill work in this book.

If you are using a computer, remember that your primary concern will be the standard typewriter keyboard. Depending upon the depth of the storage capacity of your text editor, it is important that you set aside a sufficient number of diskettes with files already created for use in your practice so that you will not have to waste valuable practice time in creating a file. On the other hand, it is important that you obtain facility in your ability to create new files quickly and to follow the menu on your diskette.

Margin Setting

When setting your margins, keep in mind that you want to get half of the key strokes to the left of the center of the paper and half of the keystrokes to the right of the center of the paper. Determine the center point of your machine and set your right margin 35 spaces to the right of it and set your left margin 35 spaces to the left of it, and you will have a line which allows 70 spaces. This includes keystrokes and blank spaces.

Your Readiness

Now that your work area and machine are prepared, it is time to concentrate on your readiness. Positioning yourself properly is a major part of organizing well. The key to mastery of any skill is mastery of the fundamentals. Correct position at the keyboard is fundamental to gaining high speeds and maintaining accurate copy. With your hips placed well back in the chair, sit with your body centered opposite the "J" key about eight inches from the keyboard. Hold your head erect, facing the copy. With your body bent slightly forward, keep your back straight and your feet firmly planted on the floor. To achieve proper balance, place one foot slightly ahead of the other, allowing six or seven inches between your ankles. Do not cross your legs.

Hand and Finger Positions

Keep your palms low, but do not allow them to rest on the frame of the keyboard. Your hands should be flat and level. The fingers should be curved and upright, resting lightly on the home row. Proper finger curvature saves motion and increases speed. Keep your forearms level with the keyboard, wrists low, but never touching the frame. Keep your thumb above the center of the space bar. Keep your fingernails cut short. Keep your arms and elbows near the body. Your elbows should be relaxed and pointing toward the floor. Remember: Do not arch the wrists, or let them rest on the frame.

Keyboard/Keystroking Review

Start to work in the right way from the beginning so that the right way will become a habit. Perhaps you have been habitually repeating a number of keyboarding processes in the wrong way. You will want to correct your form as much as possible in your practice.

The single most important of techniques is proper finger placement and reaching. Carefully study the drawing of the keyboard on this page. Note the proper finger positions. Your fingers must follow these paths at all times. Failure to do so will hinder your progress.

The most important shortcut to speed is to master the fundamentals at the outset. Technique mastery is a matter of concentration and practice.

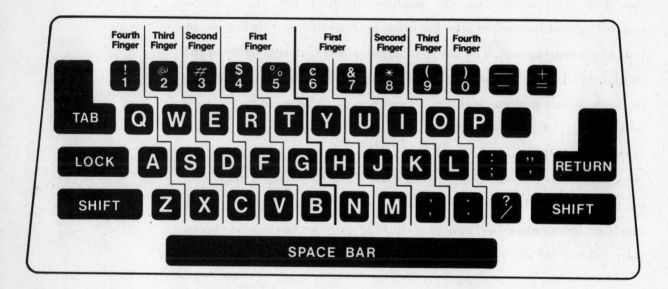

Striking the Keys

Correct fingering is a key to success at high speed and accuracy rates. In the early sessions, acquire the best form you can muster. The modern keyboard is not banked and is highly sensitive to touch. The keys are closer together, both vertically and horizontally. There are no stair steps to climb, no long reaches to make. The new keyboards require *fingering*, not striking as the old manual typewriters do. This lighter touch frees the new typist to fly lightly over the keyboard.

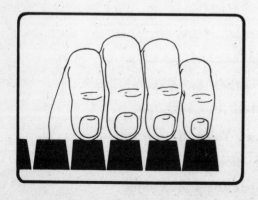
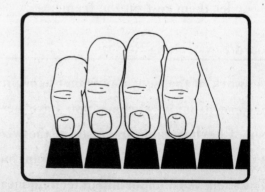

With curved, upright fingers, flick the keys, pulling the fingers toward you, and then quickly return to home row position. Flick the keys with your finger tips without moving your arms or wrist. Keep your elbows relaxed, pointing toward the floor, and in, close to your body. To achieve greater speed and accuracy, curve your fingers under when making downward reaches without moving your hands at all. Do not raise your finger from the key to strike it. Use a quick, downward action, bouncing quickly back to starting position.

Control and proper use of the space bar is as important as the use of any other key on the board. On the modern keyboard, you may hold your thumb on, or very close to, the space bar when you are typing. Do not move your fingers or wrist when fingering the space bar. Use a down-and-in motion, releasing quickly.

Space, shift, and return without pause before or after striking these keys. Operate the shift keys without wasting time or motion. When fingering reaches between key rows, don't move your hands forward for the upward reaches or downward for the lower reaches. Keep the action in your fingers. You will save time and motion by using the space bar properly.

The ability to keyboard by touch is essential. Keyboarding by touch means keyboarding without looking away from your copy, without looking at your keys. It means that you have memorized the entire letter, number, and special-character keyboard.

There are three levels of keystroking to master: (1) The keystroke, or control, level where you memorize the keyboard keystroke by keystroke, using the best finger-motion techniques you know; (2) the exploration level where you abandon accuracy momentarily to stretch your fingers to new speed highs; (3) the optimum level where you type fast, and with control, at a rate just under your top speed. This is your comfortable rate.

In early practice sessions, concentrate on the initial steps of readiness as outlined here until you have honed them to precise, automatic execution. The fastest keyboarders execute start-up routines in a few precise seconds. They finger the return key quickly, without looking up. Use firm, sharp, brisk fingering. Develop speed by fingering your keys smoothly, rhythmically, and continuously. Keep your eyes on your copy; don't look at your paper, don't look at your screen. DO NOT CORRECT ERRORS DURING THE DRILLS! Achieve rhythm as you stroke the keys.

PRETEST

Before beginning this pretest, set your tabulator for a five-space paragraph indention. It is good practice to keep your tabulator set for paragraph indention. Depression of the tabulator key counts as one keystroke.

This pretest will allow you to determine your current speed (gross words per minute—gwpm) and the number of errors you are making. Keep a record of your highest gwpm for each exercise in order to judge your progress. It will also determine which practice session you begin with. You will need a timer.

Figuring Your Speed

To figure your speed, divide the total number of strokes and spaces keyboarded by the total number of minutes typed. Every five characters or spaces keystroked are counted as one word. You may count the total number of characters and spaces in any copy, divide them by five and get the total number of words in that copy. To figure your gwpm, divide the number of words keystroked by the number of minutes typed. Keep a record of the words per minute and the number of errors you made when scoring a timed writing.

To adequately measure your gwpm, you must type for the entire time allotted. If you finish the material before your timer signals stop, repeat the copy, trying to type it through as many times as you can before the timer sounds.

Take three, 3-minute timed writings on the very easy paragraphs below. Figure your speed.

To assist you in figuring your speed, the Timed Writing Drills will show a cumulative word count at the end of each line. Below the last line in most of the drills is a scale (in parentheses) that shows the word count at the 5-, 10-, and 15-word points in the line. Look at the example below:

```
Cultivating speed with control requires consistent practice.          (12)

It is not easy, but it is rewarding.   Practice makes perfect.        (24)

                 (5)                                  (10)
```

If you completed the first line above in 1 minute, you typed 12 gwpm. If you completed both lines, you typed 24 gwpm per minute. If you are typing for more than one minute, you divide by the total number of minutes typed. On a 3-minute timed writing you might complete both lines, and get to the word "rewarding" a third time before the timer goes off. You will add $24 + 24 + 5 = 53$ and divide by $3 = 18$. You are typing at a rate of 18 gwpm.

Proofread with care, finding all of the words you mistype. Practice two lines of each of these mistyped words before taking the next timed writing.

Three-Minute Timed Writing

I see by the report that you sent me on May 5th, that you plan to (13)

lay off some of your office staff in an effort to cut your budget. I (26)

would like to have a chance to discuss this with you before you go (39)

farther. In the same report I see, too, that you want to cut down on (52)

the help in the stock room. I am in favor of this and want to help you (66)

all I can. Be sure to let me know when there is something I can do to (80)

help.You should check with Joe Vaughn at Barkleys. They have one of the (94)

most modern stock rooms in the city. We suggest that you get in touch (108)

with him to see what they can tell you about their operation. We do (121)

agree that these changes need to be made, but we wonder if your target (136)

of September 25 is a bit early. Call me as soon as you get this letter, (150)

so that we can set a day and time to meet. (158)

We need to meet as soon as we can, since we do want you to move on (171)

these new plans as soon as possible. In our meeting we will take a (185)

close look at just what you need from us to get this thing off the (198)

ground. It will be important for you to keep me posted on how things (212)

are moving along. You are doing a fine job. Keep up the good work. (226)

(5)   (10)

If your highest score is 25 gwpm or more, with 6 errors or less, you
are ready to proceed to the Speed Review on p. 28.

If your score was 24 gwpm or below with 7 errors or more, begin
with the Basic Keyboard Review Practice Sessions on pp. 23–27.

BASIC PUNCTUATION

Know these basic rules before beginning the practice sessions.

- When a period marks the end of a sentence, space twice after it by fingering the space bar twice in quick succession. If the end of the sentence occurs at the end of a line, do not space after it.
- When a period follows an abbreviation or an initial, space once after it.
- When a question mark (?) or an exclamation point (!) marks the end of a sentence, space twice after it. If it occurs in a sentence, space once after it.
- Always space twice after a colon.
- Leave no space between a quotation mark and the first or last letter in the quotation.
- Do not space before or following a hyphen.
- Space once after a comma.
- Leave no space between a dash and the words it separates.
- Leave no space between parentheses and the words they surround.

BASIC KEYBOARD REVIEW PRACTICE 1

In this section, work on perfecting the techniques discussed above. Keyboard this easy material at a slow, comfortable rate, and don't time yourself. Use these drills lines to master proper technique, concentrating on proper finger motions and keeping your eyes on the copy. Achieve rhythm by typing at the keystroke level: See the character, say the character and keystroke it with a quick, flicking motion. Remember to pull toward yourself. Set your machine for single spacing. Type each line twice, double-spacing between the pairs by quickly flicking the return key twice, and returning to home row without looking away from your copy.

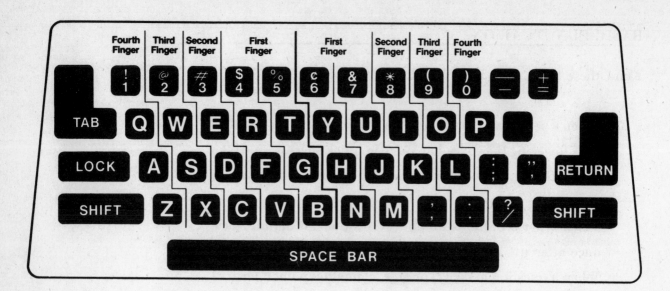

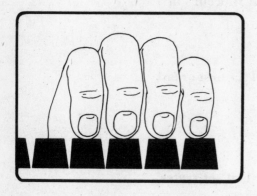
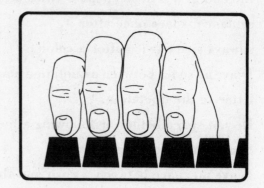

Home Row Review

gasdf hjkl; gasdf hjkl; gasdf hjkl; gasdf hjkl; gasdf hjkl;

gg hh aa ;; ss ll dd kk ff gg hh aa ;; ss ll dd kk ff gg hh

all gall dall sall fall galldall sallfall all gall all gall

aall jall kall lall ;all aa;; jall kall lall ;all aall jall

sad lad dad had kad fad jad sad lad dad had kad fad jad sad

asdf jkl; asdf jkl; asdf jkl; asdf jkl; asdf jkl; asdf jkl;

Number Review

11 22 33 44 55 66 77 88 99 00 11 22 33 44 55 66 77 88 99

12 13 14 15 16 17 18 19 20 12 13 14 15 16 17 18 19 20 12

21 22 23 24 25 26 27 28 29 30 21 23 24 25 26 27 28 29 20

31 32 33 34 35 36 37 38 39 40 31 32 34 35 37 38 39 31 32

41 42 43 44 45 46 47 48 49 50 41 42 43 44 45 46 47 48 49

51 52 53 54 55 56 57 58 59 60 51 52 53 55 56 57 58 59 60

61 62 63 64 65 66 67 68 69 70 61 62 63 64 65 67 68 69 70

71 72 73 74 75 76 78 79 80 71 72 73 74 75 76 78 79 80 71

81 82 83 84 85 86 87 88 89 90 81 82 83 84 85 86 87 88 89

91 92 93 94 95 96 97 98 99 100 91 92 93 94 95 97 98 99 100

Symbol Review

$1 $2 $3 $4 $5 $6 $7 $8 $9 $10 $1 $2 $3 $4 $5 $6 $7 $8

1&9 2&8 3&7 4&6 5&5 6&4 7&3 8&2 9&1 1&9 2&8 3&7 4&6 5&5

10% 20% 30% 40% 50% 60% 70% 80% 90% 100% 10% 20% 30% 40%

#10 #11 #12 #13 #14 #15 #16 #17 #18 #19 #20 #10 #11 #12

"a" af" "a" af" aj" "K" "l" ";" "a2 af" "a" af" aj" "k"

(a) (s) (d) (f) (j) (k) (L) (;) (a) (s) (d) (f) (j) (k)

ASDF JKL: ASDF JKL: ASDF ASDF JKL:

;'; ;'; K'K K'K ;'; ;'; K'K K'K ;'; ;'; K'K K'K ;'; ;';

1-1 2-1 3-1 4-1 5-1 6-1 7-1 8-1 9-1 10-1 1-1 2-1 3-1 4-1

10¢ 20¢ 30¢ 40¢ 50¢ ½¢ 1/4¢ 10¢ 20¢ 30¢ 40¢ 50¢ ½¢ 1/4¢ 10¢

Review

a;sldkfjgh a;sLDK fjgh a;sLDKFjgh a;sLdKfjgh a;sLdkfjgh

abcdefhgij abcdefghij abcdefghij abcdefghij abcdefghij

1223 23343445 5667 6778 7889 8990 1223 2334 3445

$10 $20 $30 4% 5% 6% #7 #8 #9 $10 $20 $30 4% 5% 6% #7 #8

adb cdd e&f "g" "h" "j" "k" "l" adb cdd e&f "g" "h" "j"

Basic Keyboard Review Practice 2

hj hj hj has hash lash dash fash hails hj hj hj has hash

ed ed ed led fled led flare sell sake led sled ed ed ed

he hed led lad sled seek seeks safe deal he had led lad

he hed led lad sled seek seeks safe deal he had led lad

ik ik if if is is hik hif his like like lake ik ik if if

tf ti te teu tie let take tall the that the tf tf ti ik

ik tf ik tf ti tis fit let fet sit if it is if he ik tf ik

dcd dcd dcd cd cd call calf call clad call dcd dcd dcd

ol ol old old fold cold lold ol ol so cold cold ol ol old

rf rf rol rol roll roll roc rock rock roll roll rf rf rol

ZA ZA ZA AZA AZA AZA haze jazz size zeal ZA ZA ZA AZA AZA

jnj jnj jnj nj nj nj an and can hand hand jnj jnj jnj jnj

uj uj uj juj uju juj due cue fan nut uj uj uj juj juj juj

ws ws ws sws sws wit wit wit wild ws ws ws sws sws

bf bf lwf buf fib fib fib fib bf bf bf lwf buf fib fib

YJ YJ YJ JYJ JYJ JYJ you you your your your Yj Yj Yj JYJ

```
ys xsxs six six Fix Fix Fox Fox jinx jink ys xsxs six six

UF UF Ufvieview save salvesicoelive have UF UF UFvieview

p; p; p; pad pad paid pen spend spent paid prize p;p; pad
```

Keyboard each of the paragraphs below twice.

```
    Just one year ago today you opened an account with us:  This is a

suitable time to express our thanks for your friendship as well as your

business.  Serving you has been a pleasure.  All of us here hope that you

will always find a helping hand in our store.

    You can hear almost anything you want to hear about the unbelievable

speed of new office copiers.  Claims range from 75 to 140 or more copies a

minute.  The new 235 makes 89 good, clean copies a minute, and works for

weeks without a stop.

    We are pleased to reserve our bridal suite for June 23 to 27.  Please

plan to arrive after 4 p.m. and forward a deposit of $193 to hold the suite.

We look forward to serving you and wish you a life of wonderful years

together.
```

Use this basic review of the keyboard and touch-typing to build a solid platform from which to reach for your highest speed and accuracy potential. When you have comfortably mastered the drill lines above you are ready to proceed to the Speed Development section.

T W O

SPEED DEVELOPMENT

SPEED REVIEW

As you practice each of the drill lines below, achieve rhythm by keyboarding at the keystroke level. See the character, say the character and keystroke it with a quick, flicking motion, remembering to pull toward yourself. The second time you key the drill line, concentrate on maintaining good form, but push for a faster rate.

Type the easy lines as fast as you can, allowing your fingers to fly over the keys. Exercise control and concentrate on technique on the more difficult lines. Each time you type a line, try to finger it faster than the time before.

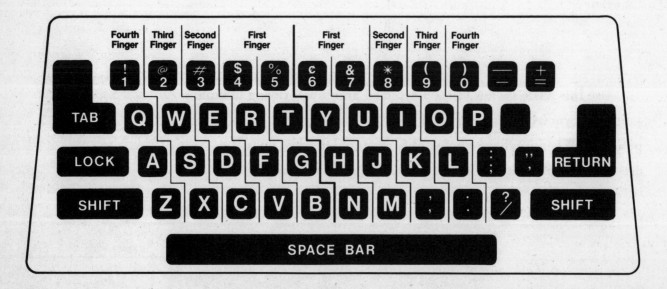

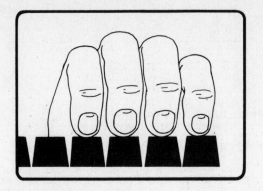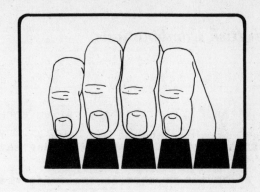

Develop rhythmic keystroking patterns. Rhythmic keystroking is striking each key with equal force. It means training your fingers to follow the same path for each stroke. Curve your fingers under for downward reaches like d/c, or j/m.

Practice drill lines at your own rate, searching for higher speed levels. Timed writings and speed bursts will be clearly marked and that is the only time you need to set your timer. The following symbol marks all timed tests:

Notice your hand movement: Keep the action centered in the fingers. Avoid any motion of your hands. Do not lift them off the keyboard for any reason. Keep your eyes on the copy, your wrists relaxed, but never touching the frame. Use the correct fingers, maintain good posture, type by touch. Concentration produces optimal keystroking. Remember: The key to mastery of any skill is mastery of the fundamentals.

Type each line twice, single-spaced. Double-space between the pairs by depressing the return key twice.

Alternate Hands

```
may for big did the and rug due fit got eye lap oak dot pry pal girl

fork dozen live tight thus leak shelf world emblem handle tutor paid

pal digit dismay local those cities idle corn clay pry pal dot their
```

High-Risk Combinations

a/s

assault ascend ascribe ascot atlas ashamed asset asbestos askance

salary stake squads snap snafu snag savor savory savvy Saxony sax

King Atlas was smashed in the spine when the space ship squad assaulted him.

d/e

fed led lent debt death feed dent den density dense deny depart dept.

educate edict bed head editor edit edify edifice ecumenical eddy dear

The education of the demure demon was meant to demean the dentist.

Reaches

When reaching from one row of keys to another, do not return to the home row. Develop a rhythmic keystroking pattern. Rhythmic keystroking means flicking the keys evenly. Keep your eyes on the copy. Keep your arms and wrists motionless. Flick the keys with your finger tips.

even late curb dude much dark tear paid eyes fries ties buys

fund voice must understand prize junked continue pretend win

Mary rotated the intervals between her files with great success.

Words and Phrases

Focus on these short words and phrases as a unit. Read, think, and type them as a whole.

we me it in an is am to my by do up at us or of be

as he if so no go it is us at be to do or ox go if

act for old odd due bag man may got new try pen nap

aid ask hay did two has had sir she sit six was way

Sentence Practice

Type each sentence twice, single-spaced. Double-space between the pairs.

```
Please send the package by express mail.

The book, The Fire Next Time, is fine reading.

"The Purple People Eater" is a new television series of note.

As soon as you receive this letter, please forward the merchandise.

The new office supply order contains a specific request for #2 pencils.

But the expense report #.907 was a fraud.  The company auditors acted with

dispatch in reporting the matter.
```

Paragraph Practice

Key the paragraph below twice. Set your tabulator key to indent the first sentence of the paragraph by five spaces. Do not use your space bar to indent. You are wasting valuable time and motion when you do so.

```
     The best typists make reaches from top to bottom rows without stopping

on home row keys.  These experts train their fingers to follow the same path

for each stroke, each time the key is fingered.  These first-rate

professionals keep their eyes on the copy.  They have trained their fingers

not to slant or touch.
```

Speed Evaluation

Now that you have completed the speed review drills, it is time to evaluate your speed. Timing your gwpm rate will be integral to the remaining work in this book. Use a timer for all timed writings. You may use the sort of timer found in kitchens. They are often sold in the housewares sections of department stores. Do not use a watch or clock, since looking up to pay attention to the sweep of the second hand or the rotation of the digits will distract your concentration. Until you are able to obtain a timer, ask someone to time you. It is good practice to read all material through before keyboarding. This familiarity with the copy will aid your keystroking.

ERROR LIMIT: 7–9

SPEED RANGE: 25–30

 Read the following paragraphs carefully for meaning. Take three, 2-minute timed writings on the following material. Try to increase your speed with each timing.

Typing fast with accuracy is a matter of concentration and practice.   **(14)**

If you wish to increase your speed, it is necessary to practice daily. The   **(30)**

longer your practice session the more skill you will gain. But, if you've   **(45)**

been away from the keyboard for sometime, it may take several sessions for   **(60)**

you to build up stamina. Do not practice for more than two hours in any one   **(76)**

session.   **(84)**

 Take two, 2-timings on the following paragraph. Use correct fingering. Keep your eyes on the copy, and sit erectly with your feet placed squarely on the floor. Use the cumulative word count at the end of the line and the cumulative word count below the paragraph to figure your speed. Divide the total number of words typed by 2.

To develop speed let your fingers fly over the keyboard, remembering   **(14)**

that the new typist fingers keys lightly. To develop accuracy, concentrate   **(29)**

on and practice the best patterns you can muster. The most important   **(43)**

shortcut to high speed is to master the basics at the outset. You will need   **(58)**

to evaluate your practice sessions to determine how well you adhere to the   **(73)** technique goals. When striving for speed, don't worry about errors: Let your   **(88)**

fingers fly over the keys. Never stop to correct errors during practice   **(103)**

drills or timed writings.   **(108)**

(5)   **(10)**

PRACTICE SESSION 1

You are aware that concentration is the cornerstone skill for professional keyboarders—or for any finely honed skill. In the next few practice sessions you will concentrate on speed, letting your fingers fly across the keyboard. Naturally, you want to exercise enough control to avoid making excessive errors. Nevertheless, your primary focus will be on speed. The goal of this section is to develop maximum fingering speeds in minimum time. While you will not concentrate on accuracy you will be aware of what constitutes too many errors.

Concentrating first and foremost on proper technique, you must push yourself to maximum speeds without loss of control. Regularity and continuity of practice are of utmost importance to these sessions. When you miss a practice session you lose some of your progress. It is best to build up momentum and then work on sustaining it.

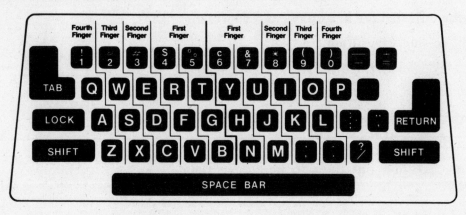

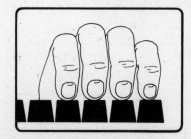
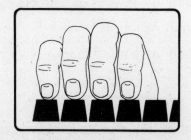

Constant self-evaluation is essential. You must assess your attitude and performance as regularly as your practice. We all have good and bad days, so do not be overly self-critical when you don't do too well. Resolve to do better in the next session. When you know you've given your best effort under the circumstances, commend yourself, and look forward to greater progress the next time. Set a specific improvement goal each day.

As you work your way through the following drills, push for greater speed on each line. If you find yourself out of control, slow down to "see it, say it, finger it" levels and gradually work up. Concentrate on using quick, snappy fingering. Finger each key with equal force. Strive for smooth, steady, finger-reach action, keeping your hands and arms quiet. Speed up on easy words and phrases; finger harder words at a slower pace.

If you wish to sustain long, productive periods of keyboarding the proper positioning of your hands, body, and feet are major factors.

Review the technique checklist below.

- My work area is well organized and free of unneeded objects.
- My work area is well lit.
- My machine is properly set for margins, line spacing, tabulation, and paper alignment.
- My monitor has been adjusted for brightness and contrast.
- I am beginning this session when I am fresh.
- My head is erect, my back straight, and my body leans slightly forward.
- I am properly centered at the machine.
- My feet are flat on the floor, apart, and in front of me.
- My wrist and palms are low, but they do not touch the machine.
- My forearms are level with the keyboard, and my elbows are relaxed, pointing to the floor.
- My eyes are on the copy and my fingers are curved and upright.

If you answered yes to all of the above, you are ready to begin.

The emphasis of this section is on speed, and will not focus on your errors. But, it is important that you recognize them. An error is any change in a fingered word from the copy you are reading. Only one error is charged to a word. Failure to indent paragraphs at least five spaces is an error. Do not indent by depressing the space bar five times. This is a tremendous waste of time and motion. Set your tabulator key for paragraph indention before you start.

Prod yourself to reach the highest rate of speed and the greatest degree of accuracy you are capable of. Push, plateau, and push forward again. Beware: Don't try too hard; it will work against you. Work at a pace that is comfortable for you, but challenging.

Speed bursts and speed evaluation are the only drills that are timed. You will key all other drills through until you have completed all instructions. Drills like easy copy, alternating fingers, sentence and paragraph practice are not timed drills.

Type each drill line twice. Try to finger each line with greater speed than the one before. Double-space between the pairs by fingering the return key twice and returning quickly to home row.

When you have completed a practice session, proofread for errors. Since an error may be triggered by the word preceding it or by the word immediately following it, type two lines of the word before the one with the error, the word with the error, and the one following it. For example, if you make an error in the word "trees" and the word "beautiful" came before it, and "are" followed it, your two lines will look like this:

```
beautiful trees are beautiful trees are beautiful trees are beautiful

trees are beautiful trees are beautiful trees are beautiful trees are
```

Easy Words

Practice fingering these easy words as units. Flick your fingers, pulling in. Let them fly over the keyboard. Push for speed.

it is to be he me my do if or an go as of so am oh

it is to it is at it is in if it if by it is as it

the for and may can did due ago has had she old odd see ask

all saw low was pay and and how and did and can she the few

amount degree become around employ number common chance demand

object safety regard dismay anyway enough notify verify strain

Alternating Fingers

Type each line as fast as you can, but don't strain your endurance.
Check your typing position. Concentrate on smooth rhythm. Keep your
fingers curved, the tips resting lightly on home row.

would enough known quorum emblem tight panel fork also quake their

supports supplies reports convict respect discuss provide at least

will not hopes to under the deadline reserve his place all and got

to me she is they will do they can he some will of course at peace

vacation unexpected without technique justified restore prepare as

endurance emblem dismal refresh submit organize coordinate anxiety

Common Phrases

Finger these common phrases as units.

if it if it is if it is if it will if it will save time will you if

as soon as possible at once is also and may if you thank you all of

if we go it can be done they make and for by the way we are they do

please send us for them if you agree with us for which the good for

Shift Key

Finger the left shift key with your "a" finger. Keystroke the right shift key with your ";" finger. Strike the shift key firmly. Hold it down until after you strike the letter. Release it quickly and return your finger to the home row. Do not pause before or after shifting.

```
January February March April May June July August September December

Monday Tuesday Wednesday Thursday Friday Saturday Broadway Judy Bone

Dr. Fred Hudson Mr. Herb Boyd Father LaRue Drew University Grace Lee

Atlanta, Georgia Chicago, Illinois Muskogee, Oklahoma Barnum and Bee
```

Reaches

Type continuously. Do not pause between keystrokes or at the end of a line. Make the reaches between rows without pausing between rows. Type each line as quickly as you can. Drive for speed.

```
quickly neighbor argued nerve clothes quantity remain tomorrow element

squash mosque rude quiet title drills agreed entitled dimensions style

arise field orient station separate self-service movement addition fry

probable banking trapeze ornament swell account disapprove resistances
```

High-Risk Combinations

```
d/e

bed fed led used need debit edits edict credit guide slide rides pride

delay educate expedite develop desire device deadline fired hired bed

deed speed decoder evidence thanked described prescribed default ideas

ahead Clyde cried fried submitted adhere exceed proceed listed refined
```

Numbers and Special Characters

enter 444 loan #589 which *900 price (900) size $4567.23 crisis 1.000%

pipe 1782 + 82¢ love & "you will see" 31 1/4 came 360 exact 555 789-2*

The rugged #78 truck carried the bent % sign to 789 South Avenue* (8+)

Sentence Practice

Keyboard the following sentences at optimum speed, that is, at the
fastest rate you feel comfortable. Type them a second time, pushing for
the fastest rate of speed you can muster without losing control. Don't
worry about errors at this point. Never stop to correct errors when
keystroking a drill. Return without pausing at the end of a line or at the
beginning of the next. Keep your eyes on the copy. Curl your finger to
reach down to the "x" key. Reach with your fingers. Keep your forearms,
wrist, and hands motionless in a comfortable, relaxed position.

Please send us the history of the project as soon as you can.

We promise to serve your interest as well as any broker does.

Confirm the judge's passage to the crowded city of the world.

Typists who reach their goal of top speed concentrate on good form.

Our firm gave each employee a bonus. Nevertheless, some complained.

Professor Zander led Zed to the exact location of the lost article.

The Xavier Band marched with the xylophone player leading the ranks, and got

extra applause.

Speed Bursts

Always remember to set your timer before you begin fingering a timed drill. Speed bursts are short drills which allow you to practice your very fastest keystroking motion.

 Try to keyboard the first sentence twice in 15 seconds or less. Then type the second sentence twice in 20 seconds or less. Finally complete the third and then the fourth sentence twice in 30 seconds or less.

Look in the room.

Keep your hands steady.

Brace your feet firmly on the floor.

The president looks forward to welcoming you.

Speed Evaluation

ERROR LIMIT: 7

SPEED RANGE: 30+

 Always read the copy you are about to keyboard for meaning before beginning to type.

Take a 1-minute timed writing on the material below. Note your gwpm and count your errors. If you finish the paragraph before the time is up, start over again, repeating it as many times as you can. Take a 2-minute timed writing and then take two, 3-minute timed writings on the paragraphs. Proofread each timed writing. Practice two lines of each word you make an error in before going on to the next timed writing. Remember to set your timer before you begin typing.

Timed Writing

If you are making many errors in your typing, check your posture (13)
first. Many typists are surprised to see just how important good posture (27)
is. However, for most of us, fatigue is the big culprit. Your goal is (42)
to train your fingers to move along the same paths as they move from (56)
row to row and key to key. But if you are tired you will let your (69)
wrist sag, your shoulders slump, or perhaps you will squirm in your (82)
seat, changing your position. These movements will alter your finger (96)
paths. Keep in mind there is a point when practice begins to hurt you (110)
rather than help you. To force yourself to practice when tired can (124)
impede your gains. (126)

You may also find that you make many errors when you type (138)
everything at your top speed. Working at your top rate for too long a (153)
time will strain your endurance. The experts train themselves to work (167)
at rates just under the pace of the top edge of their speed. This way, (181)
when you start to tire you have a reserve to call on. It also allows (195)
you to apply a burst of speed on easy words and phrases. (206)

You should not proceed to the next practice session until you (219)
have completed all of the drills in the previous one, unless you are (233)
meeting the error and speed objectives for that session. These (246)
objectives are noted at the beginning of the timed writing. If you are (260)
unable to finish a session in the allotted time, pick up where you (273)
left off in your next session. Remember: To practice when you are tired (287)
can do more harm than good. (292)

(5)   (10)

PRACTICE SESSION 2

Review the checklist on page 34. Remember: The only timed drills are the speed bursts and the speed-evaluation drills.

Sitting comfortably, with your feet firmly placed on the floor, put your hands on your lap with the palms up. Relax your shoulders and arms. Your fingers should curl naturally. Drop your hands, allowing them to dangle at your side. Let all of the tension drain down from your neck, shoulders, and arms through your finger tips and onto the floor. Place your hands in your lap again, palms up this time. Notice the natural curve in your fingers. Place your naturally curved fingers in home position. You are ready to start.

Relax and push for speed. Do not worry about your errors and don't stop to correct them. However, if you push so hard for speed that you make excessive errors, you are not building skill. You are training your fingers to key incorrectly. When you are driving for speed, you should not feel like you are skidding on an icy road trying to regain control of your vehicle, or that you are perched precariously on the edge of a dangerous cliff. You must relax and concentrate. Pushing for new speed levels should feel like trotting easily on smooth paths, accelerating from time to time. When you attain an increased speed, sustain it for longer periods.

Follow these standard instructions for all drills: Type each line twice, double-spacing between the pairs by depressing the return key twice, quickly. Type the line faster the second time. At the end of each drill, find the troublesome words in that section, those that slow you down, cause errors, or break your rhythm. Practice two lines of these words, fingering the word just before and just after the word containing the error.

Set a realistic goal and make repeated effort on the very easy copy to achieve it. When you reach your goal, sustain it. Try to gain at least 5 gwpm per practice session.

Easy Copy

Master these commonly used words and phrases on a high, automatic (keystroke) level.

```
it it is it is as it is as you it is you will it is as you say

it can it can be it can be done it can be done now it can't be

to me to you to them to those at once in by to be go for I was

she said they said he said did you will can you have you I can
```

Alternating Fingers

```
paid spent blame dismal forge conceit personnel meeting for him

worry minute forced forget for my borne scorn suspend island to

fastest freshest foremost presentation hundreds boardrooms have


approach applaud apprehend comprehend disdain forget resolve it

compare where when whole what insofar nomination population got

bicycle tricycle salesperson congregation audience market paper

budget control cost efficiency report supplement daily chatters


The haughty social scientist from Beverly Hills placed the blame on the

ancient auditor's routine.
```

Common Phrases

Master these commonly used phrases on a high, automatic (keystroke)
level.

```
in addition to during the week as soon as possible let me know I do

in the future as early as possible in all sizes with regard to as a

a prompt reply a short notice a tight deadline a final contract its

out of town in every way more or less no doubt special sale it must

in addition to express mail overnight delivery hand delivery no fee
```

Shift Key

Finger the shift key without moving your hands from the home row or
eyes from the text. Use quick, snappy strokes. When typing a series of
capital letters, depress the shift lock key. When you have fingered all of
the characters in the series, release the shift lock by quickly keystroking
the shift key. Do not pause before or after depressing the shift lock key or
the shift key.

```
John Rae Bess Janet "C & R Wholesale Tobacco Co." Friendly Row.

*John gave the Intrepid Organization $500.00 for the #250 model.

Professor deSalle assigned the best seller BELOVED for homework.

The Mariner's Temple Baptist Church is located at 3 Hart Street.
```

Row and Finger Reaches

```
continue menu resort consort retort attest bank really scripts

usual peak ought frame diskette justify reply jurist drug port

clientele customer farmer attacking longer shorter regress add

recalled expect money grieve aggrieve raise injure disciplined
```

High-Risk Combinations

```
e/i

receive deceive either efficient diets liens reins eligible being

sufficient impatient either neither service require leisure eight

tired credit expedient illegible view retrieval retrieve seizures

lucid auxiliary minicomputer mistake ignite imagine eliminate die
```

Sentence Practice

Type these sentences following the standard instructions. Check your posture and your attitude. Finger the keys smoothly, quickly, always striving for greater speed on the next line. Keep your eyes on the copy. If you are beginning to feel tired, take a five-minute break. Have a refreshing drink. Do some deep breathing and body-stretching exercises.

```
Strike the center of the space bar with a quick down-and-in stroke.

Do not pause before or after keystroking the space bar.

Build momentum by typing each line at a slightly faster pace.

When typing the drills in SHORTCUTS TO INCREASE YOUR TYPING SPEED follow

the standard instructions unless otherwise instructed.

The standard-sized paper (8½" x 11") is sold in reams of 500 sheets.
```

Paragraph Practice

 Keyboard each paragraph through twice. Try to complete it in a shorter amount of time the second time. Practice the words you've incorrectly typed and keystroke each paragraph at a higher speed. Remember to indent five spaces by setting your tabulator key. Finger the tabulator key just as you would the return key or the shift key. Do not look away from your copy. Do not pause before or after stroking the key.

Space twice after a period at the end of a sentence by striking   (13)

the space bar twice. Remember to use a down-and-in motion. Space once   (27)

after a period following an abbreviation or an initial. When a period   (41)

comes at the end of a line, don't space after it. As you move from line   (55)

to line, build momentum by typing each line at a slightly faster pace.   (69)

The characters in the complex plot of his latest novel exhibit a   (82)

streak of impatience which leaves paramount destruction. The author   (96)

quickly acknowledges paramount destruction as potentially oxymoronic.   (110)

An oxymoron is something like, type fast with deliberation, or a pleasant   (125)

disappointment.   (128)

"Send the report by facsimile copier," Emily's boss, Ellen, told   (141)

her. "It is very important to get it there on time," Ellen continued.   (156)

"Sure thing," Emily replied. She quickly placed the floppy diskette in   (171)

the disk drive. After following the directions on her menu, Ellen   (185)

began to scroll the document for last-minute corrections.   (196)

(5)   (10)

Speed Bursts

Try to complete each of the following sentences in 10 seconds or less.
Practice each sentence several times.

Keep up the good work.

It is too late to cancel now.

The weather report is fine in northern Ontario.

You can count on his quick temper, but not on his patience.

Plan a successful venture for her and she will surely reward you

significantly.

Speed Evaluation

ERROR LIMIT: 6–7

SPEED RANGE: 30+

 Take a 1-minute timed writing on paragraph one. Key at an easy, steady clip. Take a second 1-minute timing on the paragraph pushing for speed. Practice the words you've incorrectly typed following the standard instructions. Take a 1-minute timed writing on paragraph two. Key at an easy, rhythmic rate. Take a second 1-minute timing on the second paragraph. Practice your incorrectly typed words.

 Take three, 3-minute timed writings on both paragraphs, combined. If you finish them before your time is up, start over and keep typing until your timer signals. Practice words you made errors in between each timing.

To develop speed do not worry about errors. Concentrate on   (13)

smooth fingering, reaching from key to key as rapidly as possible. To   (27)

develop accuracy, you must slow down and concentrate on letters and   (40)

syllables. You must always strive to achieve the highest form. But do   (54)

you know that there is another important feature to successful typing?   (69)

It is the practice of self-discipline. The practice of discipline is   (83)

found in successful business men and women all over the world. As a   (97)

matter of fact, it is found in successful people all over the world.   (111)

Like the best keyboarder, the polished entrepreneur knows the   (124)

importance of self-discipline. Employers prefer to hire workers who   (138)

show a history of disciplined activities. Self-discipline grows best   (152)

out of self-awareness and self-honesty. If you know what you can do,   (166)

you can easily decide how to improve upon it. You can honestly assess   (180)

what you are really capable of and set goals to achieve those limits.   (194)

```
Set high goals and strive to achieve them.  Recognize your best effort;    (209)

compliment yourself for it.  Take time to reflect upon it.  Analyze         (223)

your strengths and weaknesses.  Be honest.  Do not rationalize poor         (237)

achievement.  Be self-critical.  Set goals for your future efforts.         (251)

Remember: Repeated effort is the key to winning good typing skills.         (264)

               (5)                                    (10)
```

PRACTICE SESSION 3

You may be under pressure to master the techniques presented here in a very short time. If so, you may be building up huge amounts of tension. Unattended tension will impede your progress. Attitude is important to relieving tension, or rather, to channeling its energy. Keep a positive attitude about yourself, your goals, and the work required to achieve them.

Even if you are working at a very comfortable pace, you are more than likely building up a level of tension as you push yourself beyond current limits without losing control. Positive thinking and self-confidence are central to keeping your levels of tension down. Relax, but don't get too relaxed. You need a certain amount of tension to power your motivation.

At the beginning of each practice session, take a few moments to concentrate on relaxing. Use the relaxation exercise presented in session 2. Remember: Come to these sessions when you are refreshed. Take a few seconds to meditate on breathing deeply, as you visualize a successful workout.

Begin by typing at an easy rate. Gradually increase your speed by building it slightly on each drill line, so that when you come to the end of a session you have reached your peak goal for the day and are sustaining it.

Type the easy words in your practice copy as units. Learn them at the high, optimum level. When you encounter difficult letter combinations, slow down to see it, say it, keystroke it level. Effective keying is not achieved with even intervals between strokes. Listen to the motion of a very fast typist. You will hear the variable rhythm that flows smoothly like a river. It is not possible to type all words at the same speed. You must become so practiced that you instinctively key a word according to its own rhythmic pattern. It is like the changing rhythms of a good jazz tune. They change, they make sense, they are patterned.

Although it is acceptable when building speed to race forward at the expense of control, be mindful of excessive errors. When your eyes drift from the copy, you skip letters and lose your place. Study the purpose of each drill below before keyboarding it and set appropriate mastery goals.

Common Words

Master these words and phrases at the flash-keying, high, optimum-unit level.

```
few six who why bad sad dad cad air say see set she men man mom low

try shy too now how saw end pen pin sin den die spy pro pre shy car

lag was not par out are was the say day put can his did the our her

his him see fee buy day lay lie his him the you the did has had how
```

Alternating Fingers

```
than thus this them they that they those thou their that thought it

such hand help keep sent rent dues name half noon fire hire dire to

city goes diem firm spent duty goal make when with down rise bill I

maintain traits appear appeal solve resolve dissolve foreclose wrote

continues continuous continue different difference example disclose

remember require restrict refuse reassure reclaim respond responses
```

Common Phrases

Master these high frequency words at the unit level (typing a word as a word).

it is to do do you to do to go to it of us by us by you to the as if

is to is he is she ask him ask her ask them to do this to do that to

he did and you for him to see to set the it was if you set for it is

to do the work in the past if you own he or she it is for and so did

for that time in the event of May I? Do you? Will you? Can you? I am

Shift-Key Practice

Do not look away from your copy nor pause before or after fingering the shift key. Maintain a rhythmic flow.

The Herschel W. Fields Theater Company is touring London, Rome, and Paris.

The Dean asked Kenneth to administer Quiz #1 to Hazel X. Moses in Mexico.

And You For Him May Sit Don't Ask Come Back Sit Down Return Soon Answers.

A dozen passengers sued Air Space Cadet for bad arrangements on the Mars

Shuttle.

Finger Reaches

obey city eight assets proof copier photo issue heated debate kind most

after union bad pool were opinion agreed directions important technique

secede accede creed abate pupil pump civic vicinity handled someone has

about never being early spoke wrote severe stress defeated grave rubber

ready react request voices provoke provisions insurance policy material

travel safety joined possible banker unified elated locates special pro

The Unified Effort Pact of the Washington Employees Union is next on

the agenda of the United Workers Trade Coalition Conference.*

High-Risk Combinations

i/u

ruin suit unit suite guide build union reunion cruise audit quite quits

genius medium radius incurs inputs adieu medium tedium auditorium union

Alumni Atrium antiques beautiful premium minimum issues justice quizzes

required continuity obnoxious maximum minutes jonquil juvenile justify.

Numbers and Characters

We 22 Do 44 Try 66 Can 55 do 99 for 33 jot 77 cry 88 jump 100 can 224466

4457 2900 2237 3387 9902 0577 8899 2211 1038, 56789 99324 100,984.889936

it "it" (the) 445% for & after # give: * raise! $576 .062 = 62¢ (give 90)

*it will do: common-phrases (For Your Information) ½ @ 3/4 +9

Sentence Practice

Type each sentence below twice before going on to the next.

English skills are important to all office workers; they are of utmost

importance to typists.

An important rule to execute mechanically is to space twice after a period

(.) which comes at the end of a sentence. (But, remember: Don't strike the

space bar when the period ending the sentence also ends the line. Save that

motion to key the next character.)

Another important rule to mechanically execute is to space only once after a

period (.) which occurs after an abbreviation or an initial. For example,

when keying a name like Edna R. Brown, space only once after the period

following the initial R.

Are you losing control as you speed through these sentences, constantly
trying to achieve higher levels?

If you are, slow your pace down to the keystroke level and work upwards
gradually.

Paragraph Practice

**Sustained practice builds stamina and speed. Use this paragraph to find
a rate you can sustain. Speed is your goal. Do not worry about accuracy
at this point, but do not lose control.**

The writer is working frantically to meet the unrealistic deadline set
by the marketing people. But she is determined to meet it at all cost. She
cannot avoid recalling the adage "penny wise, and dollar foolish," as she is
straining to make it. But, on the other hand, she is very sympathetic toward
the constraints of systematic organizations. "With a bit more time, what a
fine product I could render," she muses aloud as she disentangles the day's
flurry of work. But she is determined, for in her heart she believes she is
strengthened by meeting this challenge. She believes that she is prepared by
this for greater challenges to come.

Key the following high-syllabic-intensity paragraphs as fast as you can without losing control. Let your fingers fly, searching out quick patterns.

There are literally thousands of high-frequency words--words commonly used--in the business office. Many researchers have confirmed and compiled lists of such words. New to this ancient arena of the business lexicon are words like keyboarding and keystroking. Have you ever stopped to understand the most often used definition of these words? Here is an opportunity for you to do so:

When you are recording keystrokes--inputting--you are keyboarding. When you are arranging--formatting--and typing the copy you are typewriting. Keyboarding is a part of the definition for typewriting. But typewriting goes beyond the mere manipulation of keys.

Speed Bursts

 Complete each sentence below as many times as you can in 10 seconds.

Most drugstores are opened here in New Jersey.

Let the marketing people take care of the program.

They did such a splendid job last year. Look at the figures.

Of course, as the sales figures rose under his leadership, his influence

grew.

Becoming a proficient typewriter is no easy matter. It requires the use of

your brain power.

There are numerous rules the typist must understand and drill to the optimum

level in his or her pursuit of excellence.

Take three, 30-second timed writings on the paragraph below. See how many times you can complete it.

Proofreading is the search for and correction of typographical errors in

format, grammar, spelling, word division, capitalization, and punctuation.

Proofreading is a skill that you will want to develop early.

Speed Evaluation

ERROR LIMIT: 6

SPEED RANGE: 35+

Take a 1-minute timing on each of the paragraphs below.
Take a 3-minute timing on the entire essay. Practice the
words you made errors in. Take three, 3-minute timed writings on the group of paragraphs. Push for maximum speed with control.
Try to limit your errors to no more than one per minute.

There are people who love the sun. They spend many long hours   (13)

in it. These people often arrange a large number of activities in the   (27)

sun. Some of them seek to live in climates of high sun intensity like   (41)

Florida, California, and the Caribbean. Sun lovers consume many   (55)

billions of dollars in products to protect them from the harming rays of   (69)

too much sun. Some people can take more sun than others. If you are a   (84)

sun lover, or even if you just like to get your share in the spring and   (98)

summer, it pays to know your own sun-ray tolerance and stay within its   (112)

limits.   (114)

During the month of March, a multi-faceted trade show will be   (127)

held at the Jacob Javits Center in New York. This huge complex will   (142)

host men and women from all over the world who have come to inform one   (156)

another and all potential customers of the merits of their sun-care   (169)

(5)   (10)

products. As more is learned about the effect of solar rays upon human   **(183)**

skin, a proliferation of products is developing to confront and stave   **(197)**

off any imaginable problem. Other concoctions promise to enhance   **(210)**

the benefits of the sun, while many profess to do no more than give   **(224)**

you the needed confidence to loll in the sun excessively while on a   **(237)**

winter vacation in the tropics.   **(244)**

If you are among the billions of sun lovers who inhabit this   **(256)**

planet, then you will be wise to peruse the latest literature on the   **(270)**

benefits and disadvantages of sunning your body. If you wish a highly   **(284)**

intense immersion into sun-care products, visit the 3rd ANNUAL SUNIN   **(298)**

CONFERENCE at the JAVITS CENTER. For those who are interested,   **(312)**

opportunity is available but once a year. The highly motivated make   **(326)**

maximum use of this rare opportunity by returning several times.   **(339)**

Others return every day to roam and probe the seemingly unending   **(352)**

caverns of displays.   **(356)**

Some of the displays are very unique in their presentations.   **(368)**

The most unique usually allow the patrons to participate in using the   **(382)**

displayed products. At one booth lucky men and women receive free, high-   **(397)**

fashion hair-dos from such famous names in the field as Vidal Sassoon.   **(412)**

Others had their faces made up by a classy make-up artist from   **(425)**

Hollywood's top studios. Among the most prestigious of these   **(438)**

participatory merchandise displays were the simulated beaches where   **(451)**

lucky attendees could slip into a designer bathing suit and recline for   **(465)**

hours at a time under sun lamps. These sun lovers were well protected   **(469)**

by the sun-care products displayed at that booth.   **(479)**

(5)   **(10)**

Proofread your drill lines and practice the words and lines that gave
you difficulty. Strive to master them.

T H R E E

ACCURACY DEVELOPMENT

ACCURACY REVIEW

In the previous practice sessions you have concentrated on developing good habits and reaching new levels of speed. While you have been cautioned not to go out of control, you have been advised not to worry about your errors. This was done to prevent your desire for accuracy from inhibiting your search for higher levels of speed. Now that you know your fingers can fly freely over the keyboard and remain fully under your control, it is time to practice accuracy at higher speeds.

In the next sessions you will concentrate on developing high levels of accuracy in your daily performance. Naturally, as you slow down to improve upon technique, you will lose some of your speed gain. But don't worry: It is normal to type slower when you have to concentrate on smaller segments of a difficult word or phrase. Your newly acquired speed highs are like money in the bank. You put it in; you can draw it out. You can return to those speed highs with higher levels of accuracy, if you diligently practice the upcoming sessions. Remember: To build proficiency on the typewriter keyboard requires daily practice with concentration.

Accuracy is the ability to keyboard quickly while making a minimum number of errors. Ideally, typing errors should be kept below three for every 5 minutes. There will be times when you will make more than that and other times when you will perhaps make even fewer. The important fact to remember is that the more you practice an accuracy drill, the more your control will improve.

Exert precise control over the movements of your fingers. As you work through the drills and timed writings in this section, prod yourself to concentrate, but don't be a plodder. Typists who plod along slowly trying to avoid errors, tend to make far more errors than those who type faster and exercise control.

This accuracy lesson is made up of several lines of frequently used words of high syllabic intensity. We call these Preview drill lines. Concentrate on typing each word at a pace slow enough to record it without mistake, but don't plod along. Key these difficult reaches at a slower rate than your best speed. Drill your fingers until they learn and sustain the most accurate patterns of keystroking. As you continue to concentrate on difficult patterns, you should realize a steady decrease in your errors and a steady gain in your speed.

Easy Words and Phrases

Key each line of these commonly used words and phrases twice, quickly, and without error. Do not lift hands off the keyboard.

```
to the is due them is set for it is up to you it will start to you

did quit buy much in time they met and you for him may get but far

If all of you will come into the room the show will start at once.
```

Concentration

Type these frequently used difficult words at the control (keystroke) level. Your goal is to type each word without error.

```
convenience articulate programmer irregular operations suggest revenues

enlightening expeditious stockholders mechanism requisitions characters

tranquilizer situation equipment obtainable equipped neither multimedia
```

Personnel Director Application Confirmation Registered Notations Xanadu

The grievously late arrival of shipment #5 lost the company nearly $500,298

in revenue.

The inefficiencies of the former bookkeeper resulted in an excessive number

of insufficient funds notices on our accounts #2, #7 & #11.

 Type the drill lines below two times each. Then take three, 1-minute timings on the following paragraph. Try to type for the entire minute without making an error.

PREVIEW

assigned analyze developmental reverberated innocuous disappointment

management announcement theorizing hypocrisy assigned disappointment

When the interim president assigned the new auditor to analyze the   (14)

accounts for project #2334, all were startled by the inquiry. The management (30)

for this developmental program ranked among the company's finest. This   (44)

surprising new announcement reverberated from floor to floor. People were   (59)

theorizing and theorems were tossed about. Yet, we all hoped that the report (75)

would be innocuous enough. To all of our great disappointment a most   (89)

grievous occasion of hypocrisy was exposed, and our faith was shaken.   (100)

(5)   (10)

High-Risk Combinations

Key each of the following lines two times at a controlled rate. Try to type the second line without any errors. Do several practice lines of words that give you undue trouble.

c/d

deduction indicate confidence conduct recounted encode command

decreased Candida catalogued decided proceeded decode cardiac

Timed-Paragraph Practice

 Take three, 3-minute timed writings on this easy material. Strive to type the entire time without making an error. After each timed drill, develop good proofreading habits by searching out any errors you made. Practice at least two lines of these words. Try to make fewer errors each time you take a timed drill.

We were pleased to receive your order and your note asking that we   (14)

send the sales merchandise by overnight mail and the other goods by parcel   (29)

post as soon as we can. We were also pleased to see your check for $5000.00 (45)

in full payment for your order. You are indeed one of our prized customers. (61)

I am writing this note just one hour after yours arrived to let you know that (76)

we have indeed complied with your request.   (85)

Since we are well aware that your special sale starts next week and   (100)

all of the ad copy is out, we know that you are eager to have the stock you   (115)

have already promised to your buying public. As I told you on the telephone (131)

this morning, we are going to do better than overnight mail. We are   (146)

sending all of the items you ordered by one of our salespeople who will be   (161)

working in your vicinity tomorrow. Mr. Jeff Peters will fly to Denver   (176)

tonight. Your merchandise will be on board the same flight. Upon arrival at (192)

the airport, Mr. Peters will hire a van and driver and proceed directly to   (207)

your store. Although he will arrive with the goods after store hours, you   (222)

have arranged for a special crew of overtime workers to meet him there.   (237)

I was very pleased to learn that your computer system is equipped to   (251)

receive electronic mail, and that you are receiving this letter just seconds (266)

after I encode it. Please respond at once if you have any questions.   (281)

Otherwise, the arrangements are final.   (289)

(5)   (10)

Speed and Accuracy Evaluation

Five-Minute Timed Test

 Type two lines each of the preview drill lines below at the control (keystroke) level. Type slowly enough to key each word correctly. Take three, 5-minute timings on the following report. Key difficult reaches at a slower rate than your best speed. When you feel confident with these reaches, speed up. Flash through the easy words.

ERROR LIMIT: 6

SPEED RANGE: 40+

PREVIEW

employees advantageous scenarios achievement increased security

specified management executive Harvester's Manufacturing number

Amalgamated Workers Guild scrambled threatening susceptible one

When our corporations merged we had expected increased job   (12)

security. But that turned out not to be so. Apparently a deal was made to   (28)

maintain a specified number of management and executive jobs for employees of   (44)

Harvester's Manufacturing Company. When the Amalgamated Workers Guild   (60)

threatened to file a lawsuit against our company, they scrambled to comply   (75)

with the original agreement. Our lawyers wanted to fight it in court. They   (91)

felt that it was not fair to protect the jobs of one group of employees by   (106)

threatening those of others. We sure did agree with them. Nevertheless our   (122)

conservative board of directors voted to keep out of the news by avoiding a   (137)

court battle. They found it more advantageous to lay   (153)

off discretely and quietly from among our numbers.   (159)

Never being one to become susceptible to unfounded rumors, I offered   (173)

a number of plausible scenarios to discredit this panicky story. When some   (189) approximate version of the claim appeared particularly high on the ladder of   **(205)**

the grapevine, I was astonished. "Why, ours is one of the fundamental   **(220)**

institutions of this state," I thought. "Surely this can't be true."   **(234)**

Another fear of mine is to be presumptuous; therefore, I persevere   **(248)**

against its development in my character. (Some of my friends claim that this   **(264)**

trait makes me appear wimpish.) You can imagine that it took extraordinary   **(280)**

effort on my part to decide to arrange a sort of confrontation with a well-   **(295)**

placed executive with whom I was friendly. We often had lunch together. And   **(311)**

our stops for cocktails after work were not infrequent. I knew of a little   **(326)**

place convenient to both us that served scrumptous hors d' oeuvres, and I   **(340)**

invited my friend to join me there after work, but before dinner.   **(353)**

Perhaps my decision was injudicious, but after quietly devouring the   **(367)**

tidbits on the platter before us and downing nearly a half a bottle of   **(381)**

Bordeaux I got to the point. My friend immediately became the company   **(396)**

official when I broached the subject of layoffs among us; recalling my usual   **(312)**

timidity he found no embarrassment in defending the company's decision to   **(327)**

release, nearly surreptitiously, long and faithful employees. At first I   **(342)**

thought my friend to be facetious. Slowly, very slowly, I realized how   **(358)**

serious this executive was. I could not fathom this attitude and sought   **(374)**

liberation by storming away from our table, leaving an unpaid bill.   **(388)**

(5)   **(10)**

PRACTICE SESSION 1

The fundamental skill to develop for accuracy is concentration. Concentrate on controlling the fingering patterns in each of the following drills. Each time you achieve accurate keystroking, seek to increase your speed. Always flash-type the easy words and phrases.

Easy Words and Phrases

Key these drill lines quickly, without error.

```
of the to the you did it will they can are you the problem is

on due but she it did not when both for him they agree will I

It is never too late to develop good habits if you will just try.
```

Concentration

Use the lines in this section to increase your power of concentration over difficult stroke patterns. Begin slowly and build as you gain familiarity with the pattern. Your goal is to type each line without a mistake. If you do make a mistake—remember, all typists do—don't stop until you have typed the entire drill. Proofread the completed drill and carefully find all of the words or patterns you have errors in. Try to type two correct lines of each word. In a third line, practice the word, the word before it and the one following it; then repeat the drill line the word came from.

```
abcdefghijklmnopqrstuvwxyz aa bb cc dd ee ff gg hh ii jj kk ll mm nn oo pp

qq rr ss tt uu vv ww xx yy zz AA BB CC DD EE FF GG HH II JJ KK LL MM NN OO PP

aqa ;p; sws lol ded kik frf juj gtg hyh fvf jmj hnh gbg dcd k,k sxs l.l az

necessary commitment committee therefore obtainable associations

maintenance conscientious miscellaneous exhilaration paragraphed

simultaneously nucleolus microprocessor flowchart glitch Fortran

assembler language interface magnetic executrix zucchini opinion
```

Key each of the drill lines below twice for accuracy. Then take a 1-minute timing on the paragraph below the drill lines. Proofread your copy and practice two lines of each word you made an error in. On the first line type the word before, the word containing the error, and the word following it. On the second type the word without error. Take two more 1-minute timed writings following this same process. Be a careful proof-reader! You do not want to form the habit of overlooking your mistakes.

```
reliable electronic difficulty specifications platform activation

flickering reactor corrected verification manual #7826 difficulty
```

```
     The reliable #7826 reactor had electronic difficulty this morning.  Just

as I arrived on "Platform 1A" I noticed a flickering screen.  I could just

discern the message "there is trouble on lot .0062.  *See special manual for

proper activation and (50%) verification—this done all flaws will be

corrected.  *(For further information see SPECIFICATIONS MANUAL 1238, pages

20092 to 20367.)
```

High-Risk Combinations

Concentrate as you key these easily transposed letters. Use these drill
lines to improve finger motion and to eliminate persistent errors.

```
c/d

confidence educate handicap camaraderie caducous included advanced

cadence cadaverous candid accommodate accustomed coordination cast

The exquisite calmander wood of an East Indian tree is not to be confused

with the calamondin, a spiny citrus tree of the Philippines.
```

Speed and Accuracy Evaluation

 Take three, 5-minute timed writings on the paragraphs below. Type the preview lines first. Practice words with errors
between each timed writing.

ERROR LIMIT: 5

SPEED RANGE: 40–45

PREVIEW

```
possessives? hyphenated commanders in chief, mothers-in-law fathers-in-law

John Naisbitt MEGATRENDS. (apostrophe s). originator grammarians apostrophe

obligations comprehension recognition construction associations information
```

How much do you know about plurals and possessives? When a compound   (14)

word contains a noun and is hyphenated or made up of two or more words,   (28)

the significant word takes the plural form. Study the following examples   (43)

carefully: commanders in chief, mothers-in-law, passersby, runners-up   (58)

fathers-in-law. This information should come as no surprise to articulate   (73)

office workers. Good English skills are essential to success in today's   (88)

highly competitive labor force. After all, we are the beneficiaries of the   (104)

"Information Age" according to John Naisbitt, author of the bestseller   (120)

MEGATRENDS.   (122)

Most of us know that the plural is formed by adding an "s" and the   (136)

possessive is formed by adding "'s" (apostrophe s). But are you aware that   (152)

the trend is toward omitting the apostrophe? How many times have you   (166)

noticed initials like these: CPAs. You will be wise, however, to comply   (182)

with the standard rule unless the message's originator instructs you to do   (197)

otherwise.   (199)

Here is a standard rule that sometimes confuses even the best of   (212)

grammarians. Singular nouns form the possessive by adding 's. But, when   (228)

it is awkward to add the "s" because the word already ends in that sound,   (233)

add only the apostrophe. For example: the boy's mother, but Mrs. James'   (248)

son.   (249)

Plural nouns form the possessive by adding an apostrophe when the   (263)

word ends in an "s": fans' roar. When the plural does not end in an "s"   (279)

you form its possessive by adding " 's": children's fair, alumni's room.   (294)

Joint possession is indicated by adding the possessive ending to the last   (309)

noun. For instance: Brown and Smart & Jones and Smith's obligations were   (325)

fulfilled by the published contract.   (332)

In idiomatic construction you will often use the possessive form: a   (347)

day's work, five dollars' worth, this week's meeting.   (358)

Your comprehension and recognition of proper usage cannot be   (371)

overstressed in the business office. It is important that you know the   (386)

common rules automatically, like a quick reflex. For the more difficult and   (401)

obscure ones it pays to have a good style manual handy. An often   (414)

recommended one is the manual published by the Modern Language Association.   (430)

(5)   (10)

PRACTICE SESSION 2

The purpose of the accuracy practice is to allow you to concentrate on precise stroking. Do not expect accuracy to come easily: You will have to exert your power of concentration for sustained periods of time, but earnest practice will pay a high reward. Persevere and discover that there is always a demand for good typists. Type each word at a pace slow enough to record it without mistake. Drill difficult words until you master them.

Common Words and Phrases

it be we me am my by go at as or it be we me am by go

and you for the him may bag get but far met due there

Concentration

Coordination: Contemptible: Incongruous: Precarious: Prodigious; Phenomenal:

simultaneously. irreverent. perfunctory. auspicious. dissonant. obsolete.

Speed and Accuracy Evaluation

 Take three, 5-minute timings on the following manuscript after you have keyed two lines each of the drill lines. Proofread carefully, find all of your errors, and practice several lines of each word attempting to master it.

ERROR LIMIT: 5

SPEED RANGE: 45+

PREVIEW

competent organizer particular refreshments biographical introduction

arrangements transportation preparation cassette inconsiderate while

A lot goes into the planning of successful business meetings and   (13)

conferences. When these meetings serve rather than waste the time of busy   (28)

executives and managers, usually a team of competent organizers are working (43)

behind the scene. People who know how to plan good meetings are valuable   (58)

assets in any concern.   (63)

If you are asked to help in the planning of a meeting, the first thing   (77)

you will want to know is what kind of meeting it is, its purpose, and who   (91)

will be attending. With this information you can then select a suitable   (105)

location for the gathering. Perhaps you can use the small conference room   (119)

right on your floor. Another meeting might require that you book the   (132)

executive conference room well in advance, while another might require   (144)

booking a large meeting hall in a local hotel. Get as much information about (157)

the meeting as soon as you learn of your responsibility to plan it. As soon as (170)

you have an estimate of the number of people attending, book the appropriate (183)

space.   (184)

Always be sure that the space you have reserved is adequate. Inspect it   (195) for space, lighting, ventilation, comfortable chairs and tables, lectern or   **(200)**

podium, if needed, and facilities for refreshments.   **(210)**

Perhaps you have been asked to bring in an outside speaker for the   **(225)**

occasion. Depending upon the popularity of your choice, some speakers will   **(240)**

need to be booked months in advance. Make a realistic choice when selecting   **(255)**

a speaker. Conserve valuable time by not wasting it, trying to get someone   **(270)**

who you know is booked ahead by months, especially if you have only weeks to   **(285)**

prepare. On the other hand, if you have been instructed to pull out all of   **(299)**

the stops to get this particular speaker, you will, of course, concentrate on   **(314)**

doing just that. It will pay, however, to have an alternate person in mind.   **(329)**

Now that you have booked your speaker you will need to get a copy of   **(342)**

your speaker's preferred biographical statement for use in her or his   **(356)**

introduction. If the speaker is coming from out of town you may be   **(369)**

responsible for making transportation and lodging arrangements.   **(381)**

Another aspect of meeting preparation and planning that you might find   **(395)**

yourself responsible for is preparing the agenda. An agenda is an outline of   **(410)**

the order of business to be followed during the meeting. Perhaps you will   **(425)**

need to consult with others in planning the agenda. Or, perhaps you will   **(439)**

find that it has already been set. You need only to print and disseminate   **(454)**

it. It is a good practice to send out the agenda with the notices for the   **(469)**

meeting. It is courteous to give people enough notice to fit your meeting   **(484)**

easily into their appointment calendars. It is highly inconsiderate to ask   **(499)**

busy people to schedule a meeting on very short notice. Only emergency   **(512)**

meetings should be called in this way.   **(519)**

(5)   **(10)**

Remember: When practicing words between timed writings, practice the words around the error words.

Speed Drive

Key the following lines as fast as you can without error.

from 2334 upon 2335 hand 2336 that 2337 year 2338 that 2339

turn 3445 part 3446 just 3447 have 3448 each 3448 look 3449

and but did and why boy her him joy get the put you nor win

It will take time for the cost of the last plan to show up.

Concentration

enigma pharmacy respectively thousand probably salespersons vivacious

parallel specialized memorandum miscellaneous description application

From time to time the failure of the #690 mainframe is attributable to

neglect from more than 22% of the repair people.

The Shanghai Inn is a very famous restaurant located at 389 W. 172nd Street.

It is the vexation of analyzing and perfecting difficult techniques that

tires me.

Johnson & Johnson is a famous company (at this time) in zoological trade

items.

Nearly 34½% of the *3.0005 sales items sold @ 2-for-1 prices, a regrettable

mistake made by the markers on lot #83.

A particularly collaborative process is that which exists between mentor and

learner.

Take three, 1-minute timings on the paragraph below.

The new library in our neighborhood has 89,912 books, 763 periodical	**(14)**

The new library in our neighborhood has 89,912 books, 763 periodical   **(14)**

titles, and a large reference section. Despite this, there are those who   **(29)**

complain that its shelves are sparse. These people do not recall what it was   **(45)**

like here before the new facility was opened. We had to drive into the city   **(60)**

to get any library service at all. Some people will always complain.   **(74)**

(5)   **(10)**

High-Risk Combinations

d/k

thanked keyboard provoked attacked acknowledge locked skilled weekend

marketed decked kidney unkind quickened weakened lacked cracked kinds

After darkness we cracked down on the loiterers in the hallways here.

Three-Minute Timed Writing

 Take three, 3-minute timed writings on this easy copy. Strive
to type for the entire three minutes without error. Practice
error words.

When you called me last week, you said your work with the homeless in   **(13)**

your home town takes so much of your time that you had none left for our   **(27)**

project. Of course, I am very sorry to hear this news. On the other hand, I   **(42)**

am very happy that your wonderful skills are being applied to the needs of   **(57)**

people who need them so much. It seems, then, that in view of your current   **(72)**

occupation I will need to reschedule the deadline for completing our work on   **(87)**

the drawing for the new office building in Mammoth City. I will notify Mr.   **(102)**

Brown of these changes in our plans. It should not present a problem since   **(117)**

we gave ourselves plenty of time in the first place.   **(127)**

Certainly, I am sympathetic with your desire to serve others and will **(140)** have many questions for you when we meet for lunch. Enid has expressed a **(154)** similar attitude and plans to focus her attention on client records until you **(169)** are ready to begin. In terms of the bank records we shall proceed as **(182)** planned, as well as file all of the needed city-government forms. Our **(195)** dealers in Mammoth City are very cooperative in that regard. **(206)**

You are certainly full of surprises. I would never have guessed that **(219)** the plight of the homeless in Kentucky would claim your able services. The **(234)** benefits you can bring to such work is inestimable. You are indeed a fine **(249)** individual who continues to grow right before my eyes. **(260)**

Good luck, Janet. We look forward to seeing you very soon. **(271)**

(5) **(10)**

F O U R

SPEED WITH ACCURACY

REACHING YOUR OPTIMUM LEVEL

The goal of the remaining practice sessions is to keyboard at a comfortably fast level: speed with control. This optimum rate of keystroke production should be accomplished without tension and at the highest possible speed with minimum errors.

You are making too many errors when your count exceeds one per minute. You are achieving an excellent score when you are making three or less errors per five minutes. You are doing just fine when you are keeping your error limit to one per minute.

Another goal of the following practice sessions is to develop stamina—the ability to maintain your comfortable rate for longer and longer periods of time.

PRACTICE SESSION 1

Speed with Control

 Type each drill line two times at the control level. Take three, 1-minute timed writings on the paragraph. Type the first one on the control level, attempting to type the entire minute without error. Type the second timing at the exploration level. See just how fast you can flick your fingers over the keyboard. Don't worry about errors. Now type the paragraph at the optimum level: exert speed while you exercise precision. Review your technique and type in a relaxed manner. Follow these standard instructions for all Speed with Control Drills.

PREVIEW

#2378900—45 Louisville guaranteed merchandise demonstrated New Orleans

Mr. Frederick articulate profitable arrangement 2378900--quick delivery

Your order #2378900--45 has been sent to you via a quick-delivery company (15)

we have used for many years. When we met in Louisville last week you told me (31)

how important a fast delivery was to our deal. You emphasized that the (46)

company who guaranteed fast delivery would be the company who would get your (61)

business. At that time I assured you that we could have the goods produced (76)

and the shipment out to you in 60 days or less. Well, when your merchandise (92)

arrives one week ahead of schedule you will see that you chose the right (107)

people to do business with. We are the company for you! (119)

Mr. Frederick, you were clear and articulate about your needs in this (130)

fast-growing industry. You said that after we demonstrated our ability to (145)

give you what you wanted you would meet me in New Orleans to chart our future (160)

ventures. Our travel agent has arranged for a prepaid ticket with an open (175)

booking for you. Just let me know when you are ready and I will meet you in (190)

New Orleans to discuss our business plans. Ours will be a profitable (204)

arrangement, and I look forward to meeting with you again very soon. (217)

(5)   (10)

Sustained Speed with Control

 In this drill you will practice sustaining speed with control levels for longer and longer periods of time. Set your timer for one minute and type the copy at your best rate of speed with accuracy. You should be comfortable and tension free. Practice keyboarding for 1 minute with flawless accuracy. Repeat the drill five times.

ERROR LIMIT: 0

SPEED RANGE: 50+

PREVIEW

documents requirements organization memoranda manuscript well-planned

formatting 8½" x 11" paper inventory warehouse increasingly attractive

When you think of business documents you probably think most often of   (13)

the typical business letter. You are right in one way: business letters and   (28)

inter office memoranda are by far the most common of business documents. But   (43)

do not overlook the contribution of the business report. Depending upon your   (58)

job and the requirements of your organization, you may be called on to plan a   (73)

report.   (74)

Business reports are typed in standard manuscript form. The ability to   (87)

format and keyboard attractive, well-planned copy will be one of the most   (102)

useful skills you can acquire. There are a few general rules that will aid   (117)

you in formatting nonletter business documents.   (125)

Use good quality 8½" x 11" paper. If a report is important enough to be   (131)

composed, keyboarded, and printed, it should appear on good paper. You may   (146)

consider the paper you choose for a business document just as you would   (160)

consider the appropriate form of dress for a business meeting in the   (173) executive suite or a day of inventory in the warehouse. Become familiar with **(188)**

paper quality and learn to make suitable choices for each document you **(202)**

produce. **(204)**

If the report is to be bound at the top you will need to plan a margin **(218)**

depth of 2½ inches on the first page and 1½ inches on succeeding pages. If **(232)**

the report will be bound at the left, plan a left margin of 1½ inches. If it **(245)**

will not be bound, plan a left margin of 1 inch and a right margin of 1 **(258)**

inch. Leave at least 1 inch of margin at the bottom of each page. **(271)**

Always use double-spacing when typing nonletter material, unless you **(284)**

have received very specific instructions to do otherwise. Indent and use **(299)**

single spacing for lengthy quotations. Use Arabic numerals to number all **(313)**

pages beginning with page #2. The preferred placement of your page number is **(328)**

in the center of the page in the bottom margin. For various reasons, **(341)**

however, the page numbers in reports are found in the top margin to the right **(356)**

or in the center of the page. This practice is becoming increasingly more **(371)**

acceptable. **(373)**

Center the title of the report and type it bold--solid, capital letters. **(387)**

Triple space after the title. Type subtitles on the line below the title. **(402)**

Type headings within the body of the report at the left margin. **(415)**

(5)   **(10)**

Speed Drive

Type the drill lines below as fast as you can without making an error.

we were, you quit, as you requested, it was a, now and then, shall I.

we were able; were able to do so; he will go out of town; have faith;

    Perquisites have become so common in the world of business that the word

has become shortened to perks. Perks are the extras that top employees in a

firm get. They are something like the gold-star-by-your-name in the old-

fashioned class room. Some of the common perks are a free car, membership at

an exclusive spa, and all-expenses-paid vacations for two to exotic places;

or family-fun trips to Disney World. Some top management even have use of an

airplane.

Speed and Accuracy Evaluation

 Take three, 5-minute timings on the copy below.

ERROR LIMIT: 5

SPEED RANGE: 55

    Are you aware that listening and hearing are different? That listening   **(14)**

is a skill developed by practice just like typing. Experts agree that there   **(29)**

are four causes of poor listening, and that by practicing certain principles   **(44)**

we can all become better listeners.   **(51)**

    (When you think of the role listening plays in your day-to-day affairs,   **(58)**

you might wonder just why it isn't taught as a school subject.)   **(70)**

    Let us first consider the primary causes of poor listening: **(81)**

    Heading up the list is concentration, a word you might have seen enough   **(95)**

of by now. The average person talks at a rate of 125 to 150 words a minute,   **(110)**

but the human brain can process from 400 to 800 words a minute. Because we   **(125)**

      (5)   **(10)**

talk so slowly and our brain processes so fast, our mind tends to try to   (139)

occupy its unused portion. Our thoughts wander, or we think of several   (152)

things at once, convinced that we have mastered this technique. Another use   (167)

we make of this unused brain time is interrupting our speaker. To listen   (181)

attentively we must develop the habit of concentration.   (192)

On the other hand, listening too hard is as much of a culprit as not   (205)

concentrating. When you try to remember every word a speaker utters, you   (220)

will more than likely become confused and understand little of what is being   (235)

said. Listen for the speaker's main points.   (243)

Jumping to conclusions before the speaker has finished--sometimes before   (257)

he or she has even started to speak--contributes to poor listening. Among the   (272)

more offensive forms of this bad habit is putting words in the speaker's   (286)

mouth before the speaker can say what she or he means. Enter your verbal   (300)

interactions with an open mind. Be aware of when you are jumping to   (313)

conclusions and the damage this may do to the communication process.   (326)

The fourth pitfall a good listener must avoid is focusing on the   (339)

speaker's delivery and personal appearance rather than on the substance of   (354)

his or her remarks. As a rule, we tend to judge people by how they look. To   (369)

do this can result in not listening to what they say.   (379)

You can become a better listener by taking listening seriously. Just   (382)

because you are intelligent, well educated, and of good social standing does   (397)

not mean you have learned how to listen well. Learn to resist distractions   (412)

when you need to listen actively: Passive listening is just fine when you are   (427)

listening to your favorite music while you are reading your favorite book.   (441)

Active listening occurs when it is important that you understand what you are   (456)

hearing.   (458)

Learn to suspend judgment and listen to the merits of the speaker's   (469) meaning, the substance of what he or she says. Focus your listening by   (482)

listening for the main points and the evidence of their support.   (494)

(5)   (10)

PRACTICE SESSION 2

Your attitude about the work it requires to achieve proficient levels of
keyboarding is of utmost importance. You must maintain a confident
attitude even when your progress is much slower than you desire.
Successful people keep on trying until they have reached their goals.
Don't give up.

In the following drills, concentrate on achieving your comfortable
level—your tension-free, fastest, error-free rate—and sustaining it.

Speed with Control

 Take three, 1-minute timed writings on the following material. Keyboard the following copy first at the control level,
attempting to achieve error-free copy. Then let your fingers
fly over the keys as fast as you can without regard to error, but do not fly
out of control. Type the copy a third time at a faster control pace than the
first.

Communicating word processors (WP) can send information from one machine   (15)

to another. These same transmitters of information can receive information,   (30)

too. The equipment used in communicating WPs must be compatible. This   (45)

ability is called interfacing. Some communicating word processors can   (59)

interface with computers, depending upon the sophistication of the   (72)

equipment. This ability to interface is a feature available on many text-   (87)

editors, whether they are display or nondisplay, stand-alones, or computer-   (101)

linked.   (103)

(5)   (10)

Speed Drive

Achieve maximum error-free speeds on the common words and phrases below.

```
you can; it will, Are you? Do they? Shall I? it will not, for now

for them and then to do with that when it is ready much more than it

not quite ready make an appointment I am very sorry at the same time

Will you please pay your bill at a time very close to the next date?
```

Speed and Accuracy Evaluation

 Take three, 5-minute timed writings on the copy below.
ERROR LIMIT: 5
SPEED RANGE: 55+

PREVIEW

```
EXCEL, representative Nairobi, Kenya "Collects" "pick up" "organize"

"get ready" Drano-less Nairobi head-of-state New York Times maneuvers

deftly steering boulevard delapidated bougainvilleas erratically onto
```

```
       In support of the business plan you recently received from Mr. Bert      (15)

Johnson, the enterprising young publisher of EXCEL, a first-class quarterly,     (31)

we submit the following excerpt from a recent issue.  We believe these          (46)

paragraphs are a representative sample of the quality control the publisher      (61)

exercises over the material put into print.                                     (69)

       It is a cool Sunday morning in Nairobi, Kenya, when Sheila Rule          (81)

"collects" us from the New Stanley Hotel.  "Collects" is a term Africans use    (96)

to denote "pick up," just as "organize" means to "get ready." After gulping    (111)

down some rather insipid coffee we're ready to leave for her house to          (124)
```

nterview her. But before an interview can begin there are a couple of   **(137)**

things she must do.   **(141)**

First she has to get something to unstop her kitchen sink, which is no   **(155)**

easy task in Drano-less Nairobi. She also must purchase a few pounds of meat   **(170)**

for her dogs. All of this entails a long, twisting trip to a crowded   **(183)**

shopping center where securing a parking space is as difficult as gaining an   **(198)**

audience with an African head of state. These are a few of the mundane   **(212)**

things that intrude into the "glamorous" life of a New York Times Africa   **(226)**

bureau chief.   **(228)**

Having purchased a plunger and some food for her dogs, Rule, sitting   **(241)**

behind the steering wheel on the right-hand side of the car, deftly maneuvers   **(256)**

from the parking lot onto the left-hand lane of a fast-paced boulevard. "It   **(271)**

took me a year to learn to drive British style," she says, easing past a   **(286)**

jampacked, erratically swerving "matatu"--an old dilapidated van, which serves   **(301)**

as a cheap taxi for large groups of people.   **(309)**

Shifting gears and changing lanes, Rule appears to have mastered the   **(322)**

seemingly complicated art of keeping to the "wrong side" of the road. "This   **(337)**

will be my first time on the other side of the microphone," Rule says, again   **(352)**

insinuating her reluctance to be interviewed, including a recent invitation   **(367)**

from Charlene Hunter-Gault to appear on the "McNeil-Lehrer Report."   **(379)**

Except for the lush shrubs of purple bougainvillaeas and the occasional   **(393)**

appearance of an African woman balancing a load on her head with a baby   **(407)**

strapped to her back, suburban Nairobi is not distinctive. But we are amazed   **(422)**

to discover that Ms. Rule's home, dubbed "The Gingerbread House," comes with   **(437)**

a guard and rambles in a double-tiered fashion for a lovely acre or so. The   **(452)**

correspondent's life is looking better by the moment.   **(462)**

"You'd be surprised at how inexpensive all of this is," she says, aware   **(476)** of our astonishment. This availability of cheap help in Africa would become   (491)

more dramatically evident to us during our stay in Zambia and Zimbabwe.   (505)

"The guards work eight-hour shifts," she adds, matter-of-factly. "They   (519)

are necessary around here especially since I'm on the road so much."   (532)

Untangling her two dogs and cat from between her legs, she moves quickly   (546)

to pacify them. Then we take turns plunging the clogged sink. It flows   (560)

immediately. After offering us some succulent mangoes, she is finally ready   (575)

to sit for the inevitable. You wonder why such an attractive, articulate   (590)

woman is so reluctant to be interviewed. Had she been burned in the past?   (605)

Or is there a private person of genuine shyness beneath the now bubbly   (618)

gregariousness? If her shyness is masked, her loneliness is not.   (630)

"One of the greatest challenges about this job," she begins, "is the   (643)

loneliness. It has really challenged my basic nature. I'm used to being   (657)

surrounded by people I love. But here, as a correspondent, you go someplace   (672)

and you are alone!" The "alone" is stressed as if it were a line from <u>The</u>   (686)

<u>Heart</u> <u>of</u> <u>Darkness</u>. "The loneliness and being on the road too much can really   (699)

wear on you."   (701)

(5)   (10)

Speed with Control

 Use the copy in this drill to achieve high levels of speed without error, and sustain it for longer and longer periods of time. Time yourself and see how fast you can type the copy, keeping your errors to 1 or less per minute.

You will find numbers used frequently in business documents. A review   **(13)**

of the rules for use of numbers in printed materials will be very helpful to   **(28)**

you. The following paragraphs will serve as a guide to the proper business   **(43)**

usage of numbers in business correspondence.   **(51)**

Spell out exact numbers from zero through ten (0-10), but use figures   **(64)**

for numbers above ten. For example: **(70)**

She left three jobs and one marriage in two years.   **(79)**

There are 102 shopping days before Christmas.   **(87)**

When numbers less than ten occur in the same sentence with numbers over   **(101)**

ten use figures for all of the numbers. For example: **(111)**

The 25 people in the club sat at 1 table on 3 different afternoons.   **(224)**

Spell out the figures to tell the reader you are referring to   **(236)**

approximate quantities. But use figures for exact amounts. For example: **(250)**

We expect around twenty thousand people, although the auditorium will   **(263)**

seat 22,265.   **(265)**

Since numbers in the millions or higher are sometimes difficult to   **(278)**

comprehend, it is a good idea to follow this example: 3 billion, 200 million.   **(293)**

Always spell out a number that begins a sentence: Twelve hundred apples   **(307)**

were delivered. When the number at the beginning of a sentence is a very   **(322)**

large one (i.e. 300), rearrange the wording of the sentence so that the   **(336)**

number is not the first word.   **(341)**

You will also want to spell out indefinite numbers and amounts. For   **(354)**

example, she left a few hundred pieces behind. Spell out ordinal numbers   **(368)**

unless they are used as part of a date. Use the ordinal endings "th," "st,"   **(383)**

"rd," only when the day precedes the month: She will fly in on the 21st of   **(397)**

July. You must hyphenate spelled-out numbers under one hundred.   **(409)**

Another important rule for the proper use of numbers is the one   **(422)**

governing the use of simple fractions. You are to spell out simple fractions   **(437)**

(one-third) but use figures when a whole number is involved too (6 7/8th).   **(452)**

When you use the dollar sign ($), use figures to express the sum of   **(465)**

money. Use figures also to express percentages (%); to express measurements;   **(480)**

to express numbers in an address, or any numbers that identify objects like   **(495)**

rooms, flights, floors, etc.   **(500)**

(5)   **(10)**

PRACTICE SESSION 3

The proper attitude is essential if you want to learn to type well. It takes a lot of mental discipline to learn to type accurately with speed. Practice these difficult drills until you have mastered them and watch your keyboarding proficiency grow.

Speed with Control

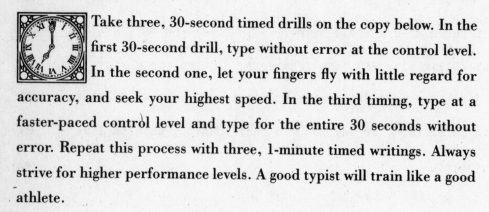 Take three, 30-second timed drills on the copy below. In the first 30-second drill, type without error at the control level. In the second one, let your fingers fly with little regard for accuracy, and seek your highest speed. In the third timing, type at a faster-paced control level and type for the entire 30 seconds without error. Repeat this process with three, 1-minute timed writings. Always strive for higher performance levels. A good typist will train like a good athlete.

```
This will confirm our telephone conversation of yesterday afternoon      (15)

wherein we agreed to meet in San Diego next month to begin the preliminary (31)

planning for the meeting.  Let me emphasize our concern here at headquarters (47)

over the sales decrease in our Northwest District #5.  I am especially happy (63)

that you are so willing to take time away from your own pressing issues to  (78)

consult with me about our concerns.                                         (85)

      On the telephone you asked why we had chosen you as the district manager (100)

we wanted to take on this special assignment.  Perhaps it would be courteous (115)

simply to say because you are a good salesperson and a very nice one, too.   (130)

But that is really a secondary reason.  The primary reason we want you to    (145)

take on leadership of the Special Task Force to Revitalize Northwest District (161)

#5 is your unmatched success as manager of that district.  We are prepared to (177)

let you write your own check.                                               (183)
```

(5)   (10)

Speed and Accuracy Evaluation

ERROR LIMIT: 3–5

SPEED RANGE: 55–60

 Practice the drill lines below and take five, 5-minute timed writings on the copy beneath them. Between each timing, type at least two lines of each word you make an error in. If you are not making the progress you desire, review your technique, tension level, and mental attitude. Are you practicing daily?

Great orators have populated every century of America's existence from (15)

George Washington to Martin Luther King, Jr. Today we are bombarded by (31)

speeches from all sorts of people on a variety of subjects. Experts remind (46)

us that speechmaking is a form of power. As a form of power, speechmaking (61)

carries heavy ethical responsibility. The use of the persuasive power of (76)

words is best used when guided by high standards of integrity. In other (91)

words, there are ethics every speechmaker should consider before taking the (106)

podium. (108)

But the members of the audience--the people listening to the speaker-- (122)

need also to develop appropriate listening skills. (132)

We are warned to consider both the worthiness of the goal of the (146)

speaker and the worthiness of the methods employed by the speaker. In other (162)

words, the means of achieving the result counts just as much as the result (177)

itself. You cannot separate the two. (185)

According to many scholars, there are at least three major ethical (199)

considerations for both speakers and listeners to keep in mind, especially (214)

where important issues are being argued. High among these requisites is (229)

the matter of knowing your subject well. The speechmaker is obligated to (244) learn as much as possible about his or her subject before attempting to   (258)

present it to others.   (262)

Strict honesty is also required of the ethical speaker. It is dishonest   (277)

to distort facts or to withold facts that do not support one's premise. The   (292)

distortation of facts and figures for self-serving reasons is reprehensible.   (308)

It is best to view each of these categories as equal parts (1/3) of a   (323)

whole concept. But if you were to attach more significance to one, the   (338)

following concern would be foremost: It is of utmost importance for every   (353)

speechmaker to use valid reasoning. A speaker may argue his or her ideas   (368)

deductively or inductively.   (374)

Deductive reasoning occurs when you reason from a general premise to a   (389)

minor one. For example: People who practice keyboarding diligently,   (403)

enthusiastically, and daily will gain in keyboard acuity. If you want to   (418)

improve your skill in typewriting, you will practice diligently,   (431)

enthusiastically, and daily. Pay close attention to a speaker's general   (445)

premise. Is it true? Is there enough evidence to support the minor premise?   (461)

Does the speaker's conclusion really follow logically from the premise?   (476)

(5)   (10)

Speed Drive

Try to type the following lines as fast as you can without making an error.
Exercise speed and control.

We are pleased to offer you the new space in our fine building.

She is one of our newest members, yet her contributions are very high.

Mr. Saxon lives at 37 Xanthus Place now. He moved from the eastside last

year.

Speed with Control

 Use the copy below to practice sustaining speed with accuracy for longer periods of time. Achieve new peaks. Take three, 3-minute timed writings on the material below. Type for accuracy during the first one; then type for speed with minimum regard for accuracy; type for control in the third. Take a fourth, 3-minute writing on this material and work for your optimum level. Type at a steady, comfortable, error-free pace. Practice the error words.

ERROR LIMIT: 3

SPEED RANGE: 50–60

```
    Perhaps you are beginning to believe that you have seen enough of the      (14)

word "skill."  For you it is tottering on falling into the useless pit of       (29)

overworked cliches.  Be careful before you kick this valuable concept over      (44)

the cliff into the murky sea of inattention.  WEBSTER'S NEW COLLEGIATE          (57)

DICTIONARY defines skill as "the ability to use one's knowledge effectively     (72)

and readily in execution or performance." Perhaps it is the weightiness of      (87)

the consideration which puts this word into such common use.  If skill is as    (102)

WEBSTER'S claims--the ability to use our knowledge effectively--it will be wise (117)

to participate willingly and even eagerly in skill-building processes through   (132)

out the duration of our lives.  It appears that to build skill banks is an      (147)

important component of human growth, development, success, and happiness.       (161)

    If you have reached this point in this book by the execution of            (171)

consecutive practice lessons aimed at improving your keyboarding skill, to      (186)

some extent you subscribe to the above.  If that is so, you will be            (199)

interested in considering the following:                                       (206)

    Although a person may acquire many highly valued technical skills, this    (220)

does not guarantee success in the world of work.  Good workers also have a     (235)
```

set of general principles governing what they do in the work place. These   **(250)**

"work skills" include the ability to be prompt, neat, and accurate. Another   **(265)**

highly valued trait is the ability to work steadily, following a task through   **(280)**

to its completion.   **(283)**

                    (5)   **(10)**

FIVE

ADVANCED PRACTICE

LETTERS AND RESUMES

Letters are perhaps the most often created of all business documents. This section will provide practice in formatting these common types of business correspondence. If you have accomplished your speed and accuracy goals, you may use this section for further practice. However, if you are well below where you would like to be, repeat the practice sessions, beginning with Speed Review on p. 28. When you reach your goal and sustain it, return to this section for further practice.

Business letters provide the core of business communications. Despite the growing popularity of the telephone as a means of business communication, final arrangements, deals, sales, and contracts are usually discussed in a letter or memo.

Business letters are typed on printed letterhead containing the company's name, complete address with zip code, and telephone number. The two most often used styles of business letters are the modified block style with mixed punctuation (this style may or may not have five-space paragraph indention) and the full block style with mixed punctuation.

The Modified Block Style Business Letter with Paragraph Indention (Mixed Punctuation)

Study the following letter. Place your dateline and set your margins for a short letter. When setting your margins for a business letter, remember that you want to achieve longer line lengths for long and two-page letters, and shorter line lengths for short- and average-length letters. The dateline and complimentary closing lines align in the modified block style letter at the center of your paper.

After you have looked the sample letter below over thoroughly, type it beginning with the date line. After you have typed the letter through once, set your timer and try to type the letter without error in five minutes or less.

```
                    THE BENJAMIN COMPANY
                       3 Jones Street
                     Detroit, MI 48204
                      (313) 577-2324

                                    March 22, 19--


Mr. Howard Abercrombie, President
Savemore Products
8181 Calvert Road
Springfield, IL 62512

Dear Mr. Abercrombie:

     As we discussed in our telephone conversation yesterday, my company is
expanding rapidly and it is likely that our needs for your very fine products
will increase.  Consequently, we are already planning for the future and
securing additional warehouse space to store the additional quantities.

     The second aspect of our growth plan for Savemore Products requires a
meeting with your people to determine the most efficient and economical plan
to get our shipments delivered on time.  We, of course, want the best deal
possible, but we also want an arrangement that you can handle comfortably.  I
am sure that we can arrive at mutually acceptable (and profitable) terms.
Please call and let me know when you would like to meet.

                              Sincerely yours,


                              Beverley Elliott, Sales Manager


ed
```

Full Block Style Letter (Mixed Punctuation)

Read the following letter and consider its placement. Arrange top and side margins to correspond with the needs of an average-length letter. Time your keystroking of the letter first at the control level, then the speed level and finally at the optimum level.

```
              HARVESTER MAGNUN INVESTMENT FIRM
                   1890 West Grand Boulevard
                    New Rochelle, NY 10012
                       (212) 924-1723


November 1, 19—


Evelyn Perkins, District Manager
Simpsom and Daily, Inc.
2381 Mobile Street, N. W.
Washington, DC 20000

Dear Ms. Perkins:

This letter is acknowledgement of the astuteness of your judgment in warning
me that not changing accounting firms at once would result in disaster for my
client, Brown & Company.  At that time we assured you that we had placed a
great deal of trust in our relationship with this firm.  In fact, their
presentation four years ago had convinced us that the data-input system they
had especially designed for the needs of this multi-million dollar account
was the best available.  Some of the very best minds in the firm attended
those meetings.

Naturally, we were hesitant to accept your analysis.  That hesitancy was
perhaps exacerbated by the fact that you informed us of this first perception
three hours after you began the audit.  During your 21-day scrutiny of our
records we were convinced that an assiduous monitoring of that account in the
upcoming days would be expeditious.  This became even more important as the
markets went into an extended period of unstable fluctuations.  By following
your advice, we were able to foresee and avert huge losses.

We would like to offer you a long-term contract to audit our records
quarterly for design accuracy.  My secretary will call you in a few days to
arrange a meeting.

Sincerely yours,


Samatha Long, Vice-President

hb
```

Occasionally the layout of your business letter will require proper placement of special notations. The following modified block style letter without paragraph indention contains examples of the most common special notations.

Review the letter, then type it through at the control rate. Type it a second time at the accuracy rate (optimum level) and finally at your optimum rate. If you type the letter through perfectly, do not type it again.

```
                         Graham Furniture Movers
                           18000 Dixie Highway
                          Milwaukee, WI 532087


                                     August 25, 19--

CONFIDENTIAL

Holcomb, Burnstein, and Swartz
Attorneys at Law
301 Lerner Park Drive
Suite 71
Highland Park, MI 48216

Attention: Lisa Ponak, Senior Partner

Ladies and Gentlemen:

SUBJECT: Case file #190-23-6784.08

We received your letter advising our firm that you were aware of a number of
potential lawsuits against our firm due to bad business practices.  You claim
that your evidence indicates that those who are proposing filing these
grievances against us will surely win in a court of law.  You go on to say
that you believe some of the charges to be so severe, and therefore so
potentially damaging to our fine reputation, that it would, indeed, be in our
best interest to arrange to meet and negotiate with you in good faith behind
closed doors.

Although we are certain that you will be unable to substantiate any charges
against our exemplary record, like you, we prefer to avoid undue publicity.
Our negotiating team will arrive in Highland Park next Monday morning,
prepared to demonstrate to you the true facts.

Sincerely yours,


Samuel Zelman, President


dd
pc Joseph Jarmon

PS We are astounded by your charges and will defeat them.
```

Proofreader's Marks and Rough Copy

Most of the material that you keyboard in a business office will not come to you in printed form like the copy here. Very often it will be handwritten and/or filled with proofreader's symbols. Study the commonly used proofreader's marks below.

delete	⌿
close up	⊃
insert copy	∧
add space	#
spell out	*sp*
indent new paragraph	⌗
no paragraph	*no* #
transpose	∪ *tr*
capitalize	≡ *cap*
lower case	/ *lc*
let stand as is	. . . . *stet*
underline	*ital*
insert punctuation	∧
insert period	⊙
move right	⌉
move left	⌊

RESUMES

A resume is an outline of your special qualifications. It should be easy to look at and easy to read. It is a statement of facts about what you have done. Use active verbs and short, simple words. Avoid use of paper that is not standard. There are many forms a resume may assume. Some include job and career objectives; others do not. Choose a resume style that best suits the needs of your job search.

Keyboard the following resume as a practice in concentration.

STAN CLYNTON SPENCE

3190 Eastern Parkway

Brooklyn, NY 11216   (718) 555-8204 (hm)

PROFESSIONAL EXPERIENCE

EQUICOR-Equitable HCA Corporation, June 1987 to Present
<u>Communications Writer</u>
Responsible for creative-concept development of customized-communications
strategies for a wide variety of national EQUICOR clients, including:

Maidenform, Inc.	Sewell Plastics
Richardson Independent School District	Marine Midland Banks, Inc.
National Tea, Inc.	State of New York

Development of copy for print and video communications designed to promote
successful benefits-plan implementation. Interface with clients, account
executives, designers, and production people.

Warren, Gorham & Lamont, Inc., October 1985 to June 1987
<u>Senior Copywriter</u>
Responsible for high volume of direct marketing and general advertising
campaigns. Training and supervision of junior writers and proofreaders.
Responsible for delegating departmental paperwork and for synthesizing
promotional ideas of new-product directors, product managers, creative
director, art director, and production department with copy group.

Marcel Dekker, Inc., January 1985 to October 1985
<u>Copywriter</u>
Responsible for promotion of medical, engineering and technical volumes, and
journals. Markets included libraries, booksellers, academicians, and
promotion through scholarly journals. Extensive proofreading and author
correspondence.

Prentice-Hall, Inc., March 1983 to January 1985
<u>Advertising Copywriter</u>
Responsible for writing of advertising pieces, book jackets, catalogs and
card decks for business and professional trade titles.

City of San Antonio, Texas, March 1980 to June 1982
<u>Promotional Specialist</u>
Coordinated publicity for city-sponsored cultural-arts program. Scheduled
press conferences, and wrote press releases and public-service announcements
for gallery openings, dance company and drama troupe performances, and
special events. Extensive interface with local media and community groups.

EDUCATION

HERBERT BERGHOF Studios, Playwriting and Acting Seminars, New York, New York
SCHOOL OF VISUAL ARTS, Advertising Copywriting Seminar, New York, New York
THE UNIVERSITY OF TEXAS, Austin
Bachelor of Journalism, magna cum laude—December 1979
UT Achievement Scholar; Assistant to the Editor, The Daily Texan

AFFILIATIONS

"Texas Exes," University of Texas Alumni Association, New York Chapter, New
York Advertising and Communications Network